GW01339914

Original title: Surf. Secrets and Curiosities

©Surf. Secrets and Curiosities, Carlos Martínez Cerdá and Víctor Martínez Cerdá, 2025

Authors: Víctor Martínez Cerdá and Carlos Martínez Cerdá (V&C Brothers)

© Cover and illustrations: V&C Brothers

Layout and design: V&C Brothers

All rights reserved.

This publication may not be reproduced, stored, recorded, or transmitted in any form or by any means, whether mechanical, photochemical, electronic, magnetic, electro-optical, by photocopying, or information retrieval systems, or any other current or future method, without prior written permission from the copyright holders.

SURF

SECRETS AND CURIOSITIES

1

Surfing is one of the oldest sporting and cultural practices in the world, with origins dating back more than a thousand years in the vast region of Polynesia.

It was born not as a sport, but as a spiritual, social, and ritual manifestation deeply rooted in the life of the Pacific island communities.

The earliest forms of surfing were practiced on islands such as Tahiti, Samoa, and above all, Hawaii, where it reached its highest cultural expression.

It was not simply about riding waves: the act of surfing was a sacred art, a direct way to connect with the ocean, which they considered a living, powerful, and often sacred entity.

In Hawaii, surfing had a deeply hierarchical and symbolic character.

Not everyone could practice it in the same way.

There was a clear distinction between social classes.

The nobility, known as the ali'i, had the privilege of using the longest and most prestigious boards, called olo, which could reach over 5 meters in length.

These boards were carved from noble woods like wiliwili or koa, and their construction was accompanied by spiritual rituals, offerings, and blessings.

Commoners, on the other hand, used shorter boards called alaia, which also required skill but did not carry the same status.

Surfing was not merely a recreational or competitive activity.

In many cases, it served to resolve disputes between clans, to attract fertility, or as part of initiation and coming-of-age rituals.

It was common for Hawaiian kings and queens to display themselves before their people riding the waves, not just for amusement, but as an affirmation of their power, dominion, and harmony with nature.

However, everything changed with the arrival of European colonizers in the 18th and 19th centuries.

The arrival of Captain James Cook in Hawaii in 1778 marked the beginning of a radical transformation of the islands.

As Christian missionaries and European traders began to settle, they introduced a new worldview that clashed deeply with Polynesian traditions.

For the Puritan missionaries, surfing was seen as an immodest, pagan, and even libertine practice, as it was sometimes performed naked and carried strong symbolic meaning.

For decades, surfing was either banned or severely discouraged.

It was one of many cultural expressions that suffered repression under colonization and the attempt to "civilize" the native peoples.

Many sacred beaches were occupied, and ancestral knowledge about how to make surfboards, read the tides, or ride a wave began to vanish.

Surf culture, like so many other native customs, stood on the brink of extinction.

It was not until the late 19th and early 20th centuries that surfing began to experience a resurgence, thanks to the cultural resistance of the Hawaiians themselves and the interest of some visitors fascinated by the tradition.

Figures like Duke Kahanamoku, an Olympic swimmer and native surfer, were key in the revival and spread of surfing as an art, a sport, and a way of life.

Duke traveled throughout the United States, Australia, and Europe in the 1920s and 1930s, demonstrating surfing and sharing its roots.

With his charisma and talent, he helped the world rediscover this ancient practice, not just as a physical activity, but as a philosophy and a way of connecting with the sea.

2

António Laureano.

The young surfer who made history by riding the largest wave ever surfed — 26.21 meters in Nazaré in October 2020 — is not simply an athletic prodigy; he is also a unique example of early dedication, family talent, and scientific passion for the ocean.

Born in Lisbon in 2003, António grew up in a family connected to the sea: his father, Ramon Laureano, is a researcher in oceanography and climatology, and it was he who introduced António at a young age to the fascinating world of giant waves.

By the age of seven, António was already riding his first waves, and before he turned fifteen, he was surfing in conditions that would be unimaginable for many adults.

His connection with Nazaré is almost spiritual.

This Portuguese town, once a quiet fishing village, became, starting in the early 2010s, the world epicenter for big wave surfing.

While veteran surfers ventured there with experience and years of training, António began to study not only the technique of tow-in surfing — where a surfer is pulled by a jet ski to reach waves too large to paddle into — but also the precise functioning of the Nazaré Canyon, marine geology, meteorology, and swell behavior.

This hybrid approach, combining athlete and scientist, allowed him to read the ocean with an unusual depth for his age.

Before setting the world record, António was already known in surfing circles for riding waves over 20 meters tall at just 16 years old.

His precociousness earned him nicknames like "the boy of the giants" or "the Mozart of big wave surfing."

But far from seeking immediate fame, he always showed discipline, humility, and a focus on the process rather than the result.

His family, especially his father, played a crucial role not only as emotional support but also as an active part in the technical analysis and the formal submission of applications to Guinness World Records.

What is most surprising about António is his maturity.

While other teenagers were scrolling through social media, he was analyzing the pressures of Nazaré's waves with physical models and training apnea techniques to hold his breath underwater for more than four minutes in case of a wipeout.

That preparation was vital on October 29, 2020, when he faced the wave that would define his legacy.

He knew it was a special day: the weather forecast, the offshore winds, the swell direction... everything pointed to epic conditions.

He surfed the wave on a special 10'8" board, designed with his technical input, and maintained control on an almost vertical drop that left the world breathless.

It took more than two years to receive the official confirmation that the wave measured 26.21 meters, but when it came, the news traveled around the globe.

Since then, António has been recognized by the international surfing community.

He has also been interviewed by global media outlets such as the BBC, Red Bull, and Surfline, and has received honors both in Portugal and at international events.

However, he has kept his routine focused on education, alternating physical training with university studies centered on marine sciences.

He has also expressed a desire to contribute to environmental education, using his story as a bridge to inspire young people about the importance of the ocean and marine science.

Among the most notable curiosities about him is that, in addition to being a surfer, he is passionate about astronomy and medieval history.

In an interview, he confessed that before going to sleep, he would often read both surf reports and chronicles about historical battles.

He has also stated that if he weren't a surfer, he would like to be an explorer or an archaeologist.

Another peculiar fact is that he prefers to train in silence, without music, and that before each big wave session, he performs a small breathing ritual inspired by techniques of Tibetan Buddhist monks.

3

Kelly Slater is, without question, the most iconic and dominant figure in the history of professional surfing.

Born on February 11, 1972, in Cocoa Beach, Florida, United States, Robert Kelly Slater burst onto the surfing scene with an explosive combination of natural talent, competitive mindset, and an almost supernatural ability to read waves.

From a very young age, he demonstrated a special connection with the ocean: by six years old he was already riding waves, and by twelve he was a recognized prospect in the youth circuits.

His rise was meteoric, but what truly set him apart was his ability to remain at the top for more than three decades, in a sport where youth, boldness, and physical fitness are critical.

Kelly Slater won his first ASP (Association of Surfing Professionals) World Title in 1992 at the age of 20, becoming the youngest world champion in history at that time.

Even more impressive is that nearly two decades later, in 2011, he won another world title at the age of 39, becoming the oldest world champion in history as well.

Between those two milestones, he accumulated a total of 11 world titles, achieved in the years 1992, 1994, 1995, 1996, 1997, 1998, 2005, 2006, 2008, 2010, and 2011.

No other surfer, male or female, has come close to matching that number, as his dominance was so overwhelming that in many tournaments he competed not only against the best of the moment but against two different generations of surfers.

But Slater is not just about numbers.

His style in the water marked a before and after: fluid lines, millimetric control, radical maneuvers with perfect aesthetics, and tactical intelligence that made him unbeatable even when ocean conditions were chaotic.

He was capable of surfing with equal mastery in small, fast, technical waves as well as in monstrous barrels at Pipeline or Teahupo'o, where the risk of death is real.

His perfectionist approach led him to train both physically and mentally like no surfer before him.

At key moments in his career, he used techniques such as mental visualization, fasting, yoga, deep apnea training, and frame-by-frame video analysis to study both his own mistakes and those of his opponents.

Slater's career is also deeply marked by his cultural influence.

He was a mainstay for years on the television series "Baywatch," playing the character Jimmy Slade, which turned him into a global pop icon beyond surfing.

He appeared in magazines, music videos, video games, and advertising campaigns for brands like Quiksilver and GoPro.

He even has a band, The Surfers, and has collaborated with artists like Jack Johnson and Eddie Vedder.

Additionally, he authored his autobiography titled Pipe Dreams, which became an international bestseller.

Outside the waves, he has been a passionate advocate for the environment and sustainable surfing.

He is the founder of Outerknown, a high-performance eco-friendly clothing brand, and has been active in ocean preservation initiatives alongside organizations such as the Surfrider Foundation and Sea Shepherd.

However, one of his most ambitious projects was the creation of the Kelly Slater Wave Company, a business that developed the most advanced artificial wave technology in the world.

In 2015, he introduced the world to his "Surf Ranch," a pool located in the middle of the California desert capable of generating perfect, tubular, and repeatable waves, revolutionizing professional training and opening the door for surfing to expand even in landlocked areas.

Among the many curiosities surrounding Slater is his obsession with perfection: he has been known to reject waves that others would consider ideal simply because they were not "exactly" what he was looking for.

He is also passionate about golf and has competed in high-level amateur tournaments.

Despite being a multimillionaire and a global celebrity, he still sometimes travels alone, carrying his own boards, and is known for his humble and straightforward attitude with fans and competitors.

He is also one of the most active surfers on social media, where he engages with followers and shares very personal thoughts on health, politics, and the environment.

As for his longevity, it is simply astounding.

In a sport that demands extreme reflexes, flexibility, and pain tolerance, Kelly Slater continued competing at the highest level well into his 50s, defeating surfers who hadn't even been born when he won his first world title.

His rivalry with surfers such as Andy Irons, Mick Fanning, Gabriel Medina, and John John Florence has been a fundamental part of the narrative of modern surfing, and every matchup against him is considered an honor by young talents.

For many, Kelly Slater is not only the greatest surfer of all time; he is also considered the most dominant athlete in the history of any individual sport.

4

In the unusual and endearing crossover between the world of surfing and the canine universe, a series of events and competitions celebrating surfing dogs have emerged over the past two decades, with the most well-known and prestigious being the Surf Dog Surf-A-Thon, held annually in Del Mar, California.

This tournament is not a joke or a novelty act, but a true competition that combines skill, training, connection with the ocean, and a deep bond between dogs and their owners.

It began as a charitable initiative organized by the Helen Woodward Animal Center, an animal rescue center, with the purpose of raising funds for the care of abandoned animals.

Since its creation, the event has gained international fame and has become a symbol of creativity, tenderness, and surfing spirit.

During the tournament, dozens of dogs of all breeds, sizes, and ages are divided into categories according to their weight (small, medium, and large) and compete by riding waves on specially adapted boards, many of which are customized with colors, special grips, and themed decorations.

Each dog is accompanied by its human guide, who pushes them toward the wave and motivates them from the shore or the water.

A panel of judges scores not only the duration of the ride but also the dog's stance, balance, attitude, expressiveness, style, and connection with the audience.

In many cases, the waves are gentle and low to ensure safety, and lifeguards are stationed in the water at all times.

Some surfing dogs have become true international celebrities for their skills, charisma, and records.

One of the most famous is Ricochet, a Californian Golden Retriever who has not only won multiple competitions but has also been a pioneer in therapeutic surfing.

Ricochet has surfed alongside autistic children, veterans with post-traumatic stress disorder, and people with reduced mobility, promoting a form of adaptive and emotional surfing.

Her connection with humans in the water has been described as deeply intuitive, and her story has been documented in books, documentaries, and news outlets around the world.

Through her surfing, Ricochet has raised over half a million dollars for charitable causes.

Another emblematic case is Abbie Girl, an Australian Kelpie mix who was rescued from a shelter before becoming a legend.

Trained by Michael Uy, she began surfing by accident and developed an astonishing ability to maintain balance even on fairly large waves.

She was recognized by the Guinness World Records as the "longest active surfing dog" and has appeared at events from California to Australia.

Her style is elegant and serene: she lowers her center of gravity, aligns her back legs, and seems to almost meditate on the board while riding the wave.

Another standout is Tillman, an English Bulldog who, although he passed away in 2015, left an indelible mark on surf culture.

Although he was better known for skateboarding, Tillman also participated in dog surfing tournaments, and his ability to stay steady on the board despite his stocky, low-slung body made him a viral sensation.

He became so popular that he was invited onto television shows like Good Morning America, signed sponsorship deals, and served as the official mascot for several sporting events.

Another notable name is Derby, a Labrador dog with a unique twist: he surfs alongside his owner dressed in superhero costumes.

Both have been recurring figures at competitions in Del Mar and other California beaches, not just because of the technical performance of the dog, who has managed to ride waves up to 15 meters long, but also because of the duo's stage charisma.

On some occasions, Derby has surfed on a shared board with other dogs, creating moments of pure collective fun.

The surfing dog phenomenon has transcended the California coast and expanded to places like Brazil, Australia, the Philippines, and the United Kingdom.

In Rio de Janeiro, similar tournaments have been organized, and on beaches like Huntington Beach, there have even been exhibitions of dogs performing maneuvers on the waves, such as slight turns or directional changes, something unimaginable just a few years ago.

There are even now specialized dog surfing schools where trainers teach dogs how to adapt to the board, overcome fear of the water, maintain balance, and respond to signals from their human guides.

5

In the heart of the Amazon rainforest, where the river flows wide, deep, and seemingly calm, one of the most extraordinary phenomena in the surfing world takes place: the Pororoca, a wave that is not born in the ocean but moves inland along the course of the Amazon River and its tributaries.

The word "Pororoca" comes from the indigenous Tupi language and means "great roar," a name that not only describes the deafening noise that precedes the wave but also the almost mythical impact it has on the landscape, animals, and humans who witness it.

This phenomenon occurs only a few times a year, mainly between February and April, when a series of very specific astronomical and geographical conditions align.

During the equinoxes, ocean tides in the Atlantic reach their peak, and saltwater begins to surge violently against the current of the Amazon River.

The pressure is so great that the ocean manages to push a large wave inland, traveling dozens of kilometers upstream.

This wave can reach heights of up to 4 meters and advance for more than 30 minutes without stopping, sweeping away everything in its path: riverbanks, vegetation, boats, and animals that fail to escape in time.

The most astonishing part is that, despite its danger, this wave has become a challenge for the world's most daring surfers.

Since the late 1990s, surfing adventurers began taking an interest in the Pororoca as a unique opportunity to surf for uninterrupted kilometers, something impossible to achieve in the ocean.

Under optimal conditions, a surfer can stay on the wave for between 30 minutes and an hour, gliding through completely wild landscapes, with trees, birds, and exotic animals just a few meters away.

It is a type of surfing that challenges not only physical balance but also concentration and mental endurance.

One of the most famous pioneers to surf the Pororoca was Brazilian surfer Picuruta Salazar, who managed to ride the wave for over 12 kilometers in 2003, in a session that went down in history as one of the longest ever recorded.

The challenge was twofold: on one hand, the wave does not behave like a predictable ocean wave but moves forward like an unstable, irregular wall, with floating branches and treacherous whirlpools; on the other hand, the natural environment is completely wild, murky waters, piranhas, snakes, crocodiles, and even jaguars in the nearby jungle.

Surfing the Pororoca is not simply a sporting act; it is a feat of survival in a majestic, primal setting.

The most iconic place for this phenomenon is the Araguari River in the Brazilian state of Amapá, although it has also been observed in the Guamá River, the Mearim River, and other branches of the Amazon system.

The noise produced by the wave can be heard up to 30 minutes before its arrival, giving surfers and locals time to prepare or flee.

In many riverside communities, the Pororoca is regarded with respect, fear, and mysticism.

Some local legends claim that it is the fury of the ocean

reclaiming its territory, or that it represents the soul of the rivers protesting the invasion of the modern world.

Despite its spectacular nature, the Pororoca has begun to be affected by human activity.

The construction of dams, deforestation, and alterations to the natural course of rivers have reduced the intensity of the phenomenon in some areas.

In fact, in the Araguari River, where international Pororoca surfing championships were held for years, the event nearly disappeared for a time due to changes in river patterns caused by agricultural and energy interventions.

For those who have had the privilege of surfing it, the Pororoca is not just a wave: it is an initiatory experience.

There are no crowds, no judges, no television cameras at every angle.

There is only you, a board, the growing roar of the water, and an ancient jungle surrounding you.

Many surfers who have ridden it say that after the Pororoca, nothing is ever the same.

It is, quite literally, riding an ancestral force that rises from the depths of the Earth and occurs just once or twice a year, in a forgotten corner of an immense continent.

A liquid miracle that turns the river into an ocean, and surfing into a form of wild poetry.

And although the Pororoca is the most famous, it is not the only wave in the world that appears only once a year.

In remote corners of the planet, there are other tidal phenomena that offer surfers a unique encounter with the impossible.

In China, for example, the famous Silver Dragon forms, a tidal bore that surges up the Qiantang River during the Mid-Autumn Festival.

It can reach speeds of up to 40 km/h and has been surfed by elite teams, although it is considered even more treacherous than the Pororoca due to its sudden violence and the proximity of urban structures.

There is also the Bono in Indonesia, specifically in the province of Sumatra, where the Kampar River produces a river tsunami several times a year during the equinox high tides.

Like the Pororoca, this wave travels several kilometers upriver and has been the focus of international competitions.

What's interesting about the Bono is that it is not only surfed but also navigated by traditional boats that use the wave's momentum to travel long distances without engines.

Another curious phenomenon occurs in the United Kingdom, on the River Severn, where a tidal bore known as the Severn Bore forms, allowing for long-distance rides and having been surfed by locals for decades, although its height rarely exceeds 2 meters.

However, what is extraordinary is the duration: surfers like Steve King have managed to ride this wave for over an hour without interruption.

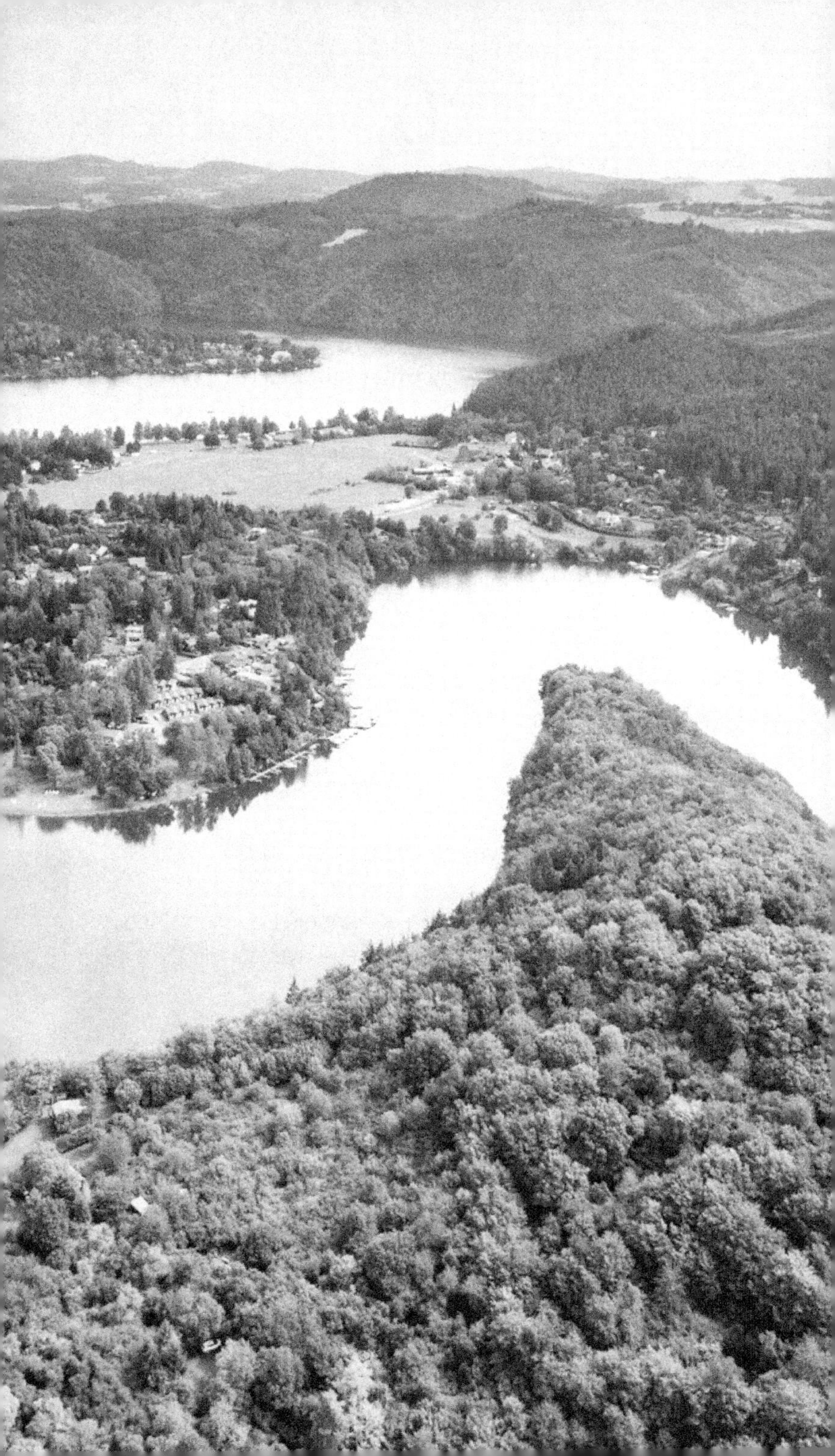

6

Bethany Hamilton is one of the most inspiring figures in the history of surfing, not only because of her talent on the waves but also because of the extraordinary resilience she demonstrated by returning to competition after an accident that would have ended the career of almost any other athlete.

She was born on February 8, 1990, in Kauai, Hawaii, one of the world's surfing meccas.

From a very young age, she grew up surrounded by the ocean and surf culture, influenced by her parents and her two brothers, all passionate surfers.

By the age of eight, she was already competing in local contests, and at nine, she signed her first sponsorship deal.

She was destined to become a professional surfing star.

But her life changed forever on October 31, 2003.

At just 13 years old, while surfing at Tunnels Beach in Kauai with her best friend Alana Blanchard, she was attacked by a tiger shark over four meters long.

The shark bit off her left arm at the shoulder, causing massive blood loss.

It was a life-or-death moment.

Her father was at the hospital awaiting knee surgery when the news arrived.

She underwent emergency surgery and survived thanks to the quick thinking of her companions and the rapid medical response.

The story moved the world, and within a few days, Bethany was known not just for her talent but for the tragedy she had faced.

What was truly extraordinary was what came next.

Instead of giving up, Bethany Hamilton decided to return to surfing.

Less than a month after the attack, she was already back in the water, and within three months, she was competing again.

She learned to paddle with one arm, to push herself powerfully from the hips, and she adapted her board with a special handle to help maintain stability.

Her first sessions were tough, but she never doubted herself.

In 2004, she won the ESPY Award for Best Female Athlete with a Disability and began competing in open divisions against able-bodied surfers, defying everyone's expectations.

In 2005, she wrote her autobiography, Soul Surfer, which became a bestseller and was later adapted into a movie.

The film *Soul Surfer*, released in 2011, tells her story in great detail and stars AnnaSophia Robb as Bethany.

Far from focusing only on the drama of the attack, the story highlights her determination, her Christian faith, her family, and her deep desire not to let her life be defined by her loss, but by her response to it.

Since then, Bethany has traveled the world as a motivational speaker, author, and media figure, always with an unbreakable smile and a serenity that has inspired millions.

In sports, Bethany has continued to achieve remarkable success.

She competed in the World Surf League, qualified for top-level championships, defeated world-class rivals such as Carissa Moore and Tyler Wright, and remained among the elite of free and competitive surfing.

In 2016, her participation in the Fiji Pro was historic: she reached the semifinals, defeating some of the best surfers in the world, all with just one arm.

Her style is characterized by incredible technical skill, strong lower body power, and a precise reading of the ocean.

Many experts have stated that beyond her personal story, her technical level places her among the best surfers in the world.

In her personal life, Bethany married Adam Dirks, a Christian educator, in 2013, and together they have built a strong, public family, having three children.

Despite her busy life as a mother and athlete, she has never abandoned her relationship with the ocean.

She continues surfing big waves, traveling to extreme locations, and pushing the boundaries of adaptive surfing.

In fact, she has promoted inclusion programs for children with disabilities, teaching them to surf as a tool for confidence and empowerment.

One of the most striking curiosities about her is her ability to surf barrels and perform advanced maneuvers without prosthetic aids.

She does not use an orthopedic arm; she accomplishes everything with her own body, using a refined technique that defies logic.

She has also developed customized surfboards, participated in big wave sessions, and taken on highly challenging spots like Jaws and Cloudbreak.

In addition, she has released documentaries such as Unstoppable, where she showcases her life without filters, her challenges as a surfer mom, and her constant pursuit of self-improvement.

7

Mark Visser is an Australian surfer known worldwide not only for taking on some of the biggest waves on the planet but for doing so under circumstances that defy all logic and safety: during the night, in complete darkness, and wearing a specially designed wetsuit equipped with LED lighting.

This feat, which catapulted him to fame, was not just a visual spectacle but a highly risky technical, mental, and physical project that combined technological innovation with an unrelenting will to explore human limits in big wave surfing.

Born in Sunshine Coast, Queensland, Australia, Mark Visser had a conventional competitive career in his early years, standing out as a talented, strong, and technical surfer.

However, he soon discovered that his true passion was not traditional competition on small or medium waves, but the almost inhuman realm of giant waves.

He dedicated himself entirely to big wave surfing, a subculture of surfing where adrenaline, preparation, and emotional control are just as important as technique.

What set him apart from other extreme surfers was not only his courage in the water but also his interest in the science of fear, mental preparation, and innovation applied to performance under extreme conditions.

In 2011, he accomplished one of the most impressive feats ever recorded in modern surfing: surfing giant waves at Jaws (Pe'ahi, on the north shore of Maui, Hawaii) in the middle of the night.

This spot is one of the most dangerous and revered locations in big wave surfing.

The waves at Jaws can exceed 15 meters (50 feet) in height and break with such brutal force that a mistake can result in severe injury or even death.

But Visser not only chose to face them, he did so under the starry sky, without natural light, guided only by an integrated LED lighting system on his suit and board, and by safety teams using night vision from jet skis and helicopters.

The project, known as Night Rider, was the result of more than two years of preparation.

Visser and his team designed a special wetsuit that incorporated high-performance LED lights, which not only allowed cameras to capture his figure among the waves but also helped him maintain orientation in an environment where the horizon line completely disappears.

He also used temperature sensors and radio communication systems to stay in contact with his team.

He trained intensely in apnea techniques to hold his breath for extended periods underwater, simulating the worst possible wipeouts.

Additionally, he subjected himself to extreme mental exercises to stay calm in total chaos.

The image of Mark Visser surfing a wall of black water, illuminated only by the bright lines of his suit and the phosphorescent foam of the waves, traveled around the world.

It was more than just a technical feat.

It was a living work of art, an extreme performance where darkness, fear, and physical mastery intertwined in a dangerous yet beautiful dance.

The feat was documented in film and television format and became an icon of what human beings are capable of achieving when they prepare physically and mentally for the impossible.

Following this achievement, Visser expanded his career in multiple directions.

He became an international speaker, author, and high-performance coach.

He has worked with Olympic athletes, elite teams, and special forces military units, teaching about fear control, performance under pressure, and decision-making in high-risk environments.

In his book The Big Wave Method, he details his comprehensive approach to mental and physical training, and how it can be applied beyond surfing, in everyday life and leadership.

He also founded the Ocean Warrior Course, a training program that combines apnea techniques, psychological resilience, and crisis situation training.

This course has been adopted by swimmers, triathletes, divers, police officers, firefighters, and rescue workers around the world, aiming to prepare individuals to act effectively in moments of intense fear or extreme conditions.

Among the most notable curiosities of his life is his fascination with the human brain under stress, leading him to collaborate with neuroscientists, psychologists, and combat trainers to understand how to stay calm when the body enters a state of panic.

He has also participated in sensory deprivation experiments, controlled drowning simulations, and hypoxia chamber training, all with the aim of perfecting his relationship with fear.

8

In the world of modern surfing, creative initiatives have emerged that reimagine the way surfboards, one of the sport's most iconic and traditional elements are made.

These new boards are not only functional, but in many cases, they also make an ethical and cultural statement: surfing cannot continue to exist in harmony with the ocean if it keeps using polluting materials such as polyurethane, fiberglass, and chemical resins, which have historically been essential to the industry.

From this spirit, extravagant and surprising creations have been born: boards made from recycled bottles, cigarette butts, coffin wood, and even human hair.

One of the leading pioneers of this movement was Australian surfer and activist Hayden Cox, creator of the Haydenshapes brand, who, along with other designers, began experimenting with sustainable materials to reduce the environmental impact of surfboard production.

But even beyond commercial proposals, artists, environmentalists, and independent surfers started to explore more radical paths.

A notable example is the boards made from recycled plastic bottles, where the cores are molded from PET plastic collected from beaches and oceans.

Although these boards are heavier than conventional ones, they have proven to be functional and have been used in exhibitions and eco-friendly tournaments as a symbol of what can be achieved with creativity and environmental commitment.

The use of recycled cigarette butts represents one of the most symbolic gestures of this movement.

Cigarette butts are among the most abundant and toxic waste found on beaches worldwide, containing highly polluting chemicals.

Some environmental organizations collected thousands of these butts, subjected them to decontamination and compression processes, and used them as the core or resin components to create boards that not only float but also tell a story.

Many of these boards, though not intended for professional use, have been exhibited in art galleries, surf museums, and eco fairs as examples of tangible activism.

Another striking example is the use of old skateboards, a natural connection between two sibling subcultures.

These boards, once no longer usable for rolling on asphalt, are recycled and pressed into layers to form the core of new surfboards.

The result is a board with a unique aesthetic, featuring colorful veins, signs of wear, and graphic elements that make them visually stunning.

The Canadian company Loaded Boards, among others, has explored this fusion between surfing and skateboarding with artisanal proposals, combining recycling, design, and functionality.

But perhaps one of the most unusual and provocative cases is that of boards made from recycled coffin wood.

This project originated in Europe as part of an artistic reflection on death, transformation, and the relationship between the body, nature, and the sea.

Coffins that were never used or were discarded due to structural defects were collected and transformed into large surfboards, many of them longboards.

The result is striking: a board built from an object associated with the end of life, now turned into a vehicle of freedom, movement, and connection with the ocean.

This type of board has sparked ethical debates but has also been praised as a symbolic way to close cycles and reuse materials that would otherwise be incinerated or buried.

Even more extravagant, some experimental brands have developed prototypes of surfboards reinforced with human hair.

This natural fiber, surprisingly strong and flexible, can be mixed with eco-friendly resins to increase durability without resorting to synthetic fibers.

This technique was inspired by studies showing that human hair, as a biological material, has properties similar to some industrial textile fibers.

The hair used comes from beauty salons and donation centers, and it is treated, sterilized, and compacted before being integrated into the core or coating of the board.

Although this type of board has not been produced on a commercial scale, it has attracted attention in sustainable design media and innovation fairs.

9

The world's largest surfboard not only broke size records but also became a symbol of community, celebration, and collective achievement in the world of surfing.

This feat took place on June 20, 2015, at Huntington Beach, California, a city known as "Surf City USA" for its historic connection to surfing in American culture.

The board, which was officially recognized by the Guinness World Records, measured exactly 42 feet long (about 12.8 meters), 11 feet wide (around 3.35 meters), and weighed over 590 kilograms.

It was specifically designed for this event, not only to float safely but also to support the weight and balance of a crowd simultaneously.

The challenge was clear: gather as many people as possible on a single wave, riding together on a colossal board without anyone falling off before the wave ended.

Such an attempt required more than enthusiasm; it demanded engineering design, buoyancy calculations, human coordination, and a perfectly synchronized ocean.

After months of preparation, the beach was filled with excitement, cameras, official judges, and thousands of spectators on the day of the attempt.

The board was carefully transported into the water with the help of heavy machinery and an impressive logistics team.

The record was finally achieved when 66 people managed to get onto the board at the same time and ride a wave for over 30 meters, standing and staying upright without falling for several seconds.

The moment was captured by drones, helicopters, and multiple ground cameras, and the resulting image — a mass of surfers riding a gigantic board in perfect harmony across the ocean — went viral within hours.

The feat not only broke the previous record, which had been set in Australia with 47 surfers on a 10-meter board, but also further solidified Huntington Beach's reputation as an epicenter for spectacular surfing events.

The board was built by a team led by legendary shaper Nev Hyman alongside naval design experts, using materials such as high-density foam, fiberglass, and a reinforced internal support structure.

It was coated with a specially formulated resin designed to withstand pressure, weight, and the salty conditions of the ocean.

Despite its titanic size, the board was engineered to maintain enough balance to avoid tipping easily, and its flat bottom helped stabilize navigation on soft but powerful waves.

The event also had a purpose beyond spectacle: it was part of the International Surfing Day celebrations and was promoted as a way to unite the global surfing community under a message of inclusion, joy, and respect for the ocean, with participants of all ages, including children, professional surfers, people with disabilities, and even veteran surfers over 70 years old.

It was, in many ways, a wave of shared humanity.

After the event, the board was preserved as a historic piece and displayed in various cultural spaces related to surfing.

It has been exhibited in museums, conventions, and sports

fairs, and has been the subject of documentaries and interviews.

For many, beyond the technical record, what remained was the feeling that surfing doesn't always have to be an individualistic or extreme feat; it can also be a collective expression, a large-scale game, a tribute to the human ability to create, coordinate, and enjoy the ocean as a community.

10

On the remote and desert coastline of Namibia, in southwest Africa, lies one of the most coveted and secret treasures of modern surfing: Skeleton Bay, considered by many surfers to be the longest wave in the world.

Discovered relatively late, in 2008, thanks to satellite images and explorations by adventurous surfers analyzing coastal formations through Google Earth, Skeleton Bay is a perfect rarity, a left-hand wave line that can stretch for more than 1.5 kilometers in a single uninterrupted break.

Its discovery revolutionized the concept of the "perfect wave" and put Namibia, a desert country without a surfing tradition, at the center of the global map of dream waves.

Skeleton Bay is a "sandbar" type wave, meaning it breaks over a sandbank, and it forms when the South Atlantic swell hits at just the right angle during the southern hemisphere's winter, generally between June and September.

The conditions must align precisely: low tides, offshore winds (from land toward the sea), and a storm in the southern ocean pushing swells toward this coast.

When this climatic miracle occurs, Skeleton Bay awakens and offers barrels lasting over a minute, with sections so fast and hollow they seem unreal.

The wave moves laterally, hugging the coastline, allowing surfers to enter endless barrels that challenge their lung capacity, balance, and reflexes.

It is a technical, extremely fast, and dangerous wave. Although it's not particularly tall (usually between 1 and 3 meters), its lateral force and suction mean that any mistake ends in a wipeout onto compacted sand, sometimes resulting in serious injuries.

Additionally, it is located in an isolated area, surrounded by dunes, shipwreck skeletons, and seal colonies.

There's no infrastructure, no lifeguards, and if a surfer gets injured, the nearest hospital can be over an hour away via dirt roads.

The experience of surfing Skeleton Bay is as much a physical adventure as it is a spiritual journey: some spend years chasing the perfect conditions for just a few seconds of perfect barrel.

Each wave there is a mixture of glory, desert dust, and reverence.

In contrast, on the other side of the planet, in French Polynesia, rises one of the most mythical and feared monsters of surfing: Teahupo'o, on the island of Tahiti.

Its name literally means "wall of skulls" in Tahitian, and it is one of the most dangerous and revered surf spots in the world.

Unlike Skeleton Bay, which is a long and navigable wave, Teahupo'o is a concentrated beast of force that breaks almost vertically over a razor-sharp coral reef, just a few centimeters below the surface.

The waves at Teahupo'o are not only massive — they can exceed 8 or 9 meters — but they are hollow, heavy, and ultra-dense, with a wall of water so thick it seems to collapse rather than break.

The most terrifying aspect of Teahupo'o is its lip: the top part of the wave doesn't just fall; it folds over itself like a mass of liquid concrete.

The volume of water moving is so immense that the wave seems to bend at a right angle, forming a perfect but deadly tube.

Surfers who dare to ride it must have nerves of steel and flawless technical preparation.

There is no margin for error.

If a surfer falls inside the barrel, they can be slammed onto the reef with such force that it causes cuts, fractures, or even loss of consciousness.

Teahupo'o has claimed multiple victims over the years, yet it continues to attract the bravest surfers on the planet.

The wave's first major media moment came in 2000 when Laird Hamilton rode a giant wave there using tow-in surfing (being towed by a jet ski), an achievement that was then considered "the most dangerous wave ever surfed."

Since then, Teahupo'o has become a regular venue for the World Surf League's Championship Tour events and will be the site of the Olympic surfing competition during the Paris 2024 Games, despite being more than 15,000 kilometers away from the official host city.

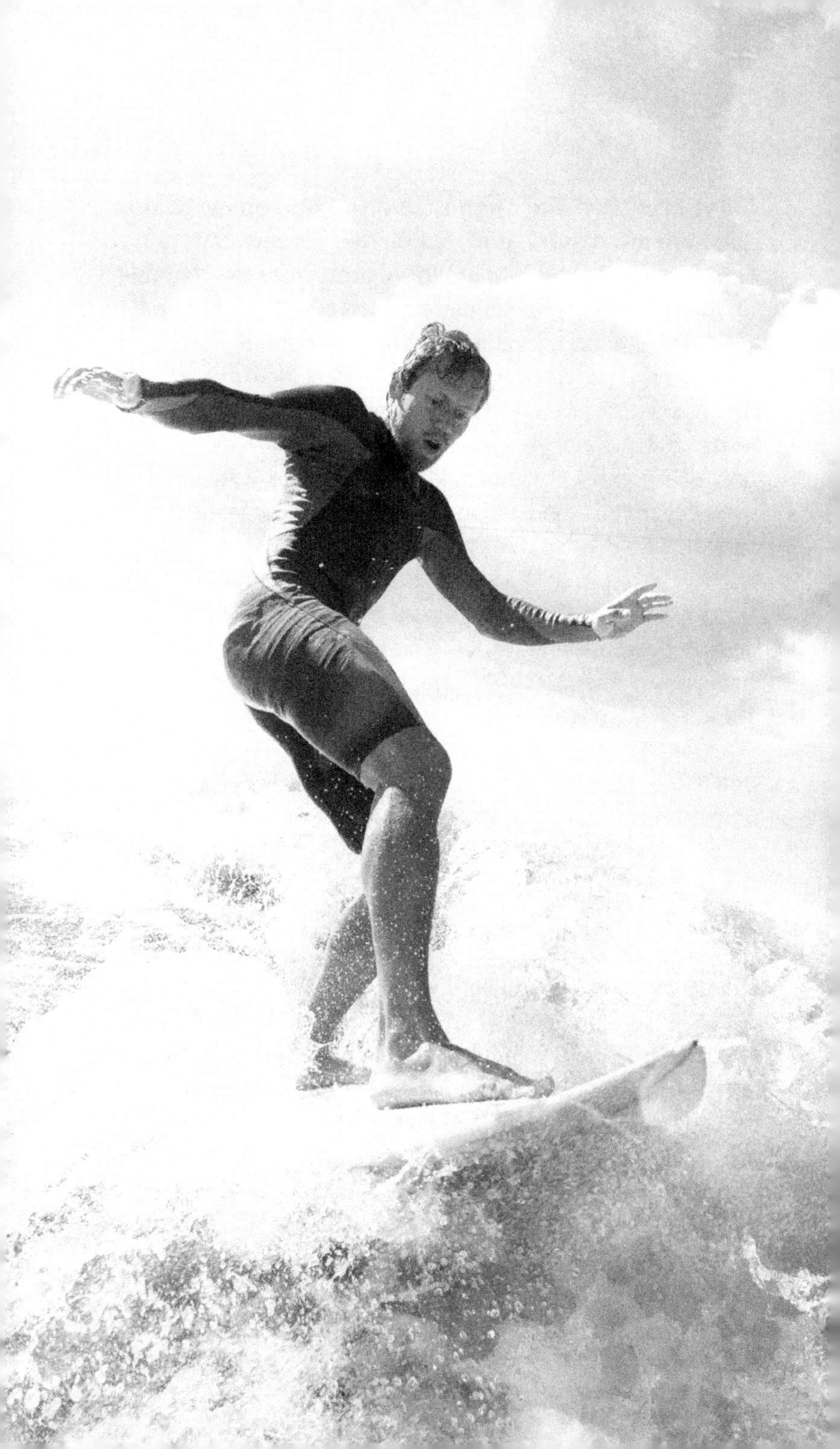

11

In the exclusive and often eccentric world of surfboards, where art, history, and technique intersect with pop culture and sustainability, there are pieces so valuable that they cease to be mere sporting equipment and become million-dollar collectibles.

The most expensive surfboards in the world are not necessarily the most technically advanced or the most functional in the water, but those that combine rarity, historical context, unusual materials, or collaborations with renowned artists.

Among them are creations painted by artists like Damien Hirst, and even allegedly by Banksy, which have driven prices easily past $100,000 and, in some cases, close to half a million dollars.

One of the most famous and expensive boards is the one Damien Hirst created as part of a series for the British art gallery Other Criteria.

Hirst, famous for his conceptual works involving animals in formaldehyde and diamond-encrusted pieces, brought his provocative style into the surf world.

He painted a board with his signature pattern of colored dots, the same style used in his "Spot Paintings" series, transforming it into a functional piece of art.

The board was produced in a limited edition of just 10 pieces and sold as contemporary artwork, not as sporting equipment.

It is a high-end board, made with premium materials, but its true value lies in the artist's signature: it has been sold at auctions for prices ranging between $60,000 and $120,000, depending on its condition and the context of the sale.

In the case of Banksy, the enigmatic British street artist known for his political and subversive art, there are no fully confirmed records of surfboards painted directly by him, but persistent rumors exist about works attributed to or inspired by his aesthetic.

Boards decorated with stencils of his most famous graffiti —such as the girl with the balloon or the protester throwing flowers— have been seen, and some have been sold at art houses with questionable certificates of authenticity, generating controversy and speculation.

Nevertheless, an original intervention by Banksy on a surfboard could easily fetch or exceed $300,000, considering that his works on canvas or walls have sold for millions.

Outside the contemporary art world, there are boards that reach astronomical prices for other reasons.

For example, antique Hawaiian surfboards made of solid wood (olo or alaia), some from the 19th or early 20th century, can reach values between $150,000 and $250,000 at private auctions, especially if associated with historical figures like Duke Kahanamoku, considered the father of modern surfing.

These boards have no fins, weigh more than 70 kilos, and were hand-carved with rudimentary tools, making them pieces of incalculable historical and cultural value.

There are also boards covered in precious materials.

The company Roy Stuart Surfboards, based in New Zealand, created the "Rampant," a surfboard made from paulownia wood, decorated with gold leaf, and equipped with a fin made of jasper.

Its starting price was $1.3 million, making it the most

expensive surfboard ever listed, although it is unknown whether it was actually sold at that price.

In this case, the goal was not water performance but rather symbolism, opulence, and collectibility.

Another line of luxury boards comes from designer Alexander Wang, who collaborated with Haydenshapes to launch an edition of surfboards featuring 3D printing, industrial black-and-white patterns, and a high-fashion aesthetic.

Although functional, their price exceeded $20,000 per board, clearly targeting a public more interested in art and design than in competition.

Interestingly, there are even boards made from recycled materials, such as ocean plastic, cigarette butts, or human hair, which, although they don't reach high prices for their materials, have been auctioned for notable sums due to their ecological message and conceptual rarity.

Some have been signed by legendary surfers like Kelly Slater, further increasing their symbolic value.

12

Duke Kahanamoku, born on August 24, 1890, in Honolulu, Hawaii, is universally recognized as the father of modern surfing, not only for his extraordinary skill on the board but also because he was responsible for bringing surfing — a practice that until then was almost exclusively Hawaiian — to the global stage.

His full name was Duke Paoa Kahinu Mokoe Hulikohola Kahanamoku, and he came from a family of noble Native Hawaiian descent.

From childhood, he lived close to the ocean, among the waves of Waikiki, and his connection to the sea was so deep that he became a legendary figure both in surfing and in swimming, a discipline in which he also left an indelible mark.

Duke was not only a pioneering surfer but also an elite Olympic swimmer.

He won his first gold medal at the 1912 Stockholm Olympics in the 100-meter freestyle, as well as a silver in the relay.

Then, at the 1920 Antwerp Games, he again captured gold in the 100 meters and in the 4x200-meter relay.

In 1924, at the age of 34, he won the silver medal in the 100 meters, demonstrating exceptional athletic longevity for his time.

His Olympic career was impressive and made him a global celebrity.

But beyond his achievements in the pool, Duke used his fame to promote surfing as a sport, an art form, and a culture.

At a time when surfing was a minority practice, almost forgotten and confined to the beaches of Hawaii, Duke revitalized it and exported it to the world.

In the early 20th century, surfing had been in danger of disappearing, repressed during the colonization of the islands by Christian missionaries, who considered it a pagan and immoral practice.

But Duke, with his elegance and charisma, restored its ancestral dignity.

He was tall, athletic, with a permanent smile, and on the board, he was poetry in motion.

He rode waves with a fluid, effortless style on large solid wooden boards called olo, some of which measured over 4 meters and weighed more than 50 kilos.

During his travels around the world as a sports ambassador, Duke brought surfing to the shores of California, Australia, New Zealand, and beyond.

In 1914, he gave a demonstration at Freshwater Beach, Sydney, which is considered the official birth of surfing in Australia.

There, he carved a board himself from local wood and showed Australians what it meant to ride a wave.

He did the same in California, where surfing took off in places like Huntington Beach and Santa Monica thanks to his influence.

He always said that surfing was more than a sport: it was a way of life, a philosophy tied to respect for the sea and the spirit of aloha, that blend of hospitality, humility, love, and connection with nature that characterizes Hawaiian culture.

In addition to his sporting contributions, Duke Kahanamoku was a charismatic and multifaceted public figure.

He appeared in Hollywood films during the 1920s and 1930s, playing exotic roles that reinforced the romantic image of the island man.

Although his roles were secondary and stereotypical, they helped maintain his presence in popular culture.

He also served as sheriff of Honolulu County for nearly 30 years, from 1932 to 1961, a position he held with widespread respect.

He was a symbol of integrity, humility, and service, becoming something of an unofficial ambassador of Hawaii to the world.

Among the most remarkable curiosities of his life is his heroism: in 1925, in California, Duke saved eight people from a shipwreck using his surfboard as a rescue device.

This feat was one of the first demonstrations of the practical value of surfing beyond sport and became an inspiration for the later widespread use of rescue boards by lifeguards.

Another fascinating detail is that, despite his fame, he lived modestly for most of his life, remaining true to his simple, generous style and his deep connection to his land and people.

He died on January 22, 1968, and his funeral was an ocean ceremony worthy of a tribal chief, with his ashes scattered in the sea at Waikiki, accompanied by dozens of Hawaiian canoes and thousands of people on the beach paying tribute to him.

Today, a bronze statue of him, with arms outstretched facing Waikiki Beach, has become a pilgrimage site for surfers from all over the world.

It is common to see flower leis around his neck or at his feet, left by people grateful for his legacy.

Duke Kahanamoku not only transformed surfing into a global sport; he brought it out of the shadows, rescued it from oblivion, returned it to the Hawaiian people, and offered it to the world as a gift.

13

Surfing, which for centuries was a spiritual, recreational, and social practice in Polynesia and today has become a global phenomenon, has transcended the realm of sport to also become a subject of academic and cultural study.

At some universities, such as San Diego State University (SDSU) and other institutions in Southern California, surfing has been formally integrated into the academic curriculum, not only from a physical standpoint but also through historical, sociological, environmental, and cultural perspectives.

This multidisciplinary approach views surfing as a window to analyze complex issues such as the relationship between humans and nature, colonialism, local identity, sustainability, cultural globalization processes, and ecological activism.

At universities like San Diego, which are geographically close to some of the world's most iconic surfing coasts, there are courses such as "Surf Culture," "The Science of Surfing," and "Oceanography and Surfing," where students learn about the physics of waves and meteorology, as well as the historical evolution of surfing and its role in social movements.

Classes may include analyses of iconic surf films, readings on surfing's economic and tourism impact, studies of the surf industry as a global phenomenon, and, in some cases, practical sessions in the ocean.

These subjects are not just intended for surfers but also for students of anthropology, environmental studies, sports science, communication, or history.

But the place where this integration of surfing, education, and culture reaches its highest expression is undoubtedly Hawaii, the birthplace of ancestral surfing.

On the islands, there are surf schools that do not simply teach how to ride a wave.

Some, especially those focused on preserving native Hawaiian identity, offer a comprehensive education that also includes the history of the Hawaiian people, traditional chanting (mele), hula dance, celestial navigation (wayfinding), the Hawaiian language ('Ōlelo Hawai'i), and cultural values such as aloha, kuleana (responsibility), and mālama (care for the land and sea).

These schools aim not just to produce technically skilled surfers, but guardians of the ocean with a profound sense of respect for Polynesian heritage.

One of the most special features of these schools is the way knowledge is passed down; it is not through conventional theoretical classes but through an experience-based, community-driven, and oral tradition pedagogy.

Many of the instructors are kumu (teachers) who have inherited knowledge from their ancestors, and each session in the water may begin with a ceremonial chant, a prayer to the ocean, or a lesson on marine genealogies.

Students are taught, for example, that waves are not just physical formations, but manifestations of energy that must be treated with reverence, and that surfing is not an act of dominance over nature but one of synchronization with it.

They also learn how to build surfboards.

Traditional techniques are preserved, with boards carved from koa or wiliwili wood without modern tools, accompanied by ritual offerings before cutting the tree, thus showing that the surfboard is seen as an extension of the body, the spirit, and the earth.

In this context, surfing becomes a sacred act that connects

the practitioner with their ancestors, the ocean, and the gods.

In some schools, surfing is even used as a form of emotional healing, especially for young Hawaiians seeking to reconnect with their cultural roots in a world dominated by tourism and modernity.

This vision of surfing as an educational vehicle has begun to influence other parts of the world and has inspired programs for therapeutic surfing, marine literacy projects, social inclusion initiatives, and coastal conservation campaigns.

14

Garrett McNamara.

He is one of the boldest and most renowned surfers in the world, and his name was forever etched into the history of surfing when, in November 2011, at Praia do Norte beach in Nazaré, Portugal, he rode a colossal wave estimated to be over 30 meters high.

Although the official measurement recognized by Guinness World Records at the time was 23.77 meters (78 feet), many argue that, given the wave conditions and later analyses, it could have exceeded 30 meters, making that session one of the most extreme and monumental feats ever achieved by a human being on a surfboard.

Garrett, born on August 10, 1967, in Pittsfield, Massachusetts, and raised in Hawaii, was already a well-known surfer for seeking out giant waves decades earlier.

His career began in the powerful waters of O'ahu, where he developed his endurance, technique, and courage surfing legendary spots like Waimea Bay.

Unlike other surfers who focused on the traditional competitive circuit, he chose the path of big wave surfing, a branch of surfing that demands a very particular relationship with fear, tow-in technique (jet-ski assisted surfing), and the physical and mental endurance to confront the ocean's wildest forces.

But his life changed radically when he was invited to Portugal to explore a new spot on the Atlantic coast that, until then, was known more for its rugged beauty than for its potential as a big wave destination.

Nazaré, a small fishing town, was hiding a secret beneath the water: the Nazaré Submarine Canyon, a geological fault over 200 kilometers long that acts as a funnel, concentrating the energy of Atlantic swells and brutally amplifying them as they reach the coast.

McNamara, along with a team of scientists, photographers, and jet ski pilots, studied the canyon, its winds, its tides, and planned a session that would change his life.

On the day of the record, Garrett was towed into the wave by his partner Andrew Cotton.

The wave was a gigantic mass of water that rose like a liquid wall from the horizon.

McNamara descended the face of the wave with surgical precision, completely glued to the surface, accelerating diagonally, and maintaining control on a board specially designed to withstand that speed and force.

The scene was captured by cameras from multiple angles, and the image of his tiny figure gliding over a blue mountain traveled around the world.

It was like watching a human riding a collapsing building.

Although the measurement was disputed — some argued that the lack of precise reference points made it impossible to verify the exact 30 meters — the impact was immediate.

McNamara appeared on magazine covers, news broadcasts, and documentaries.

His achievement put Nazaré on the world surfing map, transforming it into a must-visit destination for big wave hunters and a pilgrimage site for ocean lovers.

Since then, he has repeatedly returned to that beach himself, and has even helped train new surfers, sharing his knowledge about safety, technique, and respect for the sea.

One of the most fascinating aspects of Garrett McNamara is his spiritual approach to surfing.

For him, every wave is a form of meditation, a test of humility before nature.

He has described himself as a messenger of the sea, and has spoken openly about how waves connect him to a deeper energy that transcends the physical.

He has also participated in numerous environmental projects, using his media platform to promote ocean cleanups, education on climate change, and the protection of marine ecosystems.

In his personal life, McNamara has written an autobiography titled Hound of the Sea, where he recounts his humble beginnings, his internal struggles, his evolution as a surfer, and the most dangerous moments he has experienced in the water, including wipeouts that nearly cost him his life.

He is a family man and has tried to balance his life as an extreme athlete with his role as a husband and father, without abandoning his calling as an adventurer.

In fact, he has surfed in extreme conditions beyond Nazaré, including riding waves among icebergs in Alaska, attempts in Antarctica, and waves in completely unexplored locations.

15

**The daily training of a professional surfer
is much more demanding, comprehensive,
and varied than many might imagine.**

Far from the stereotype of the laid-back surfer who just
waits for waves on the beach, elite athletes who compete
in the World Surf League's Championship Tour or specialize
in big waves maintain routines as structured and intense as
those of any other high-performance sport.

Their daily training is designed to enhance not only
their specific skills on the board but also strength, mobility,
lung capacity, cardiovascular endurance, mental health,
and connection with the ocean.

A professional surfer's day generally starts very early, often
before sunrise, especially if ocean conditions are optimal for
training.

The first step is reviewing wave forecasts, which include
weather information, swell direction, wind speed and direction,
wave size, period between sets, and tide conditions.

This technical reading is fundamental, as it allows them
to select the right spot for the day's session and anticipate
the ocean's behavior, something that becomes an intuitive
yet scientific form of environmental reading.

Once at the beach, the surfer performs a specific physical
warm-up, which includes joint mobility exercises, muscle
activation drills, dynamic stretching, and breathing techniques.

Preparation often incorporates yoga routines or functional
ground movements that help prevent injuries, maintain
flexibility, and prepare the body for the explosiveness and

constant position changes that surfing demands.

Visualization exercises are also practiced, where the surfer mentally rehearses technical movements, maneuver lines, tube entries, or paddling techniques in critical situations.

The water session, which can last between 1 and 3 hours depending on the goal, is not simply "surfing for pleasure."

Professional surfers work on specific maneuvers such as vertical turns (top turns), precise cutbacks, aerials, tube entries, and clean exits, all under the observation of coaches or through video recordings that are later analyzed on land.

Technical repetition is key, as each maneuver must be perfected under different types of waves, speeds, and angles.

In many cases, surfers use cameras mounted on their boards, drones, or recordings from the shore to precisely analyze each movement and improve on details that might otherwise go unnoticed.

After leaving the water, many surfers perform a second physical routine focused on land-based training.

This can include functional strength work, with emphasis on core, legs, back, and shoulders, key areas for stability, board control, and power in maneuvers.

Kettlebells, TRX systems, bars, medicine balls, and, in some cases, suspension systems are used to simulate movements similar to those in surfing.

Explosiveness and reflexes are also trained using unstable platforms, balance boards, and visual reaction systems.

A vital part of the training is cardiovascular and pulmonary preparation, especially for those who face big waves.

Apnea training is done with methods inspired by freediving, including breathing tables, controlled hyperventilation, progressive breath-holding, and underwater exercises where athletes walk or swim long distances with empty lungs.

This type of training can be life-saving, as a wipeout on a wave over 10 meters high can leave a surfer underwater for more than 40 seconds, with consecutive sets preventing an immediate return to the surface.

Another essential component is nutrition, which must be perfectly balanced according to the demands of the sport.

Professional surfers often follow diets rich in healthy fats, lean proteins, vegetables, and fruits, avoiding refined sugars, alcohol, and inflammatory foods.

The goal is not only to stay in shape but also to optimize muscle recovery, maintain a strong immune system (which is crucial with changing climates and constant travel), and ensure sustained energy for long sessions.

Additionally, many surfers include mental and emotional training in their daily routine, whether through meditation techniques, mindfulness, sports coaching, or cognitive therapies.

Professional surfing, especially at the competitive level, involves high levels of pressure, constant travel, time zone changes, split-second strategic decisions, and facing fear in extreme conditions.

The mind must be as well-trained as the body to remain calm, make decisions in fractions of a second, and trust intuition, especially in giant waves where fear can be paralyzing.

In the afternoon, if ocean conditions do not allow for a second session in the water, time is used for physiotherapy sessions, cryotherapy, sports massages, or active recovery exercises like swimming in a pool, foam rolling, or walking on sand.

Videos of competitions are also analyzed, rivals are studied, wave records are reviewed, and travel is planned based on approaching swells around the world.

In this sense, surfers are almost like ocean geography scientists, tracking weather patterns, Pacific depressions, and wind rotations as part of their sports calendar.

Finally, rest is considered a fundamental pillar.

Professional surfers prioritize sleep, the quality of nighttime recovery, and stress management.

Many use tools such as biometric watches, sleep tracking apps, and digital detox strategies to ensure that both body and mind regenerate completely.

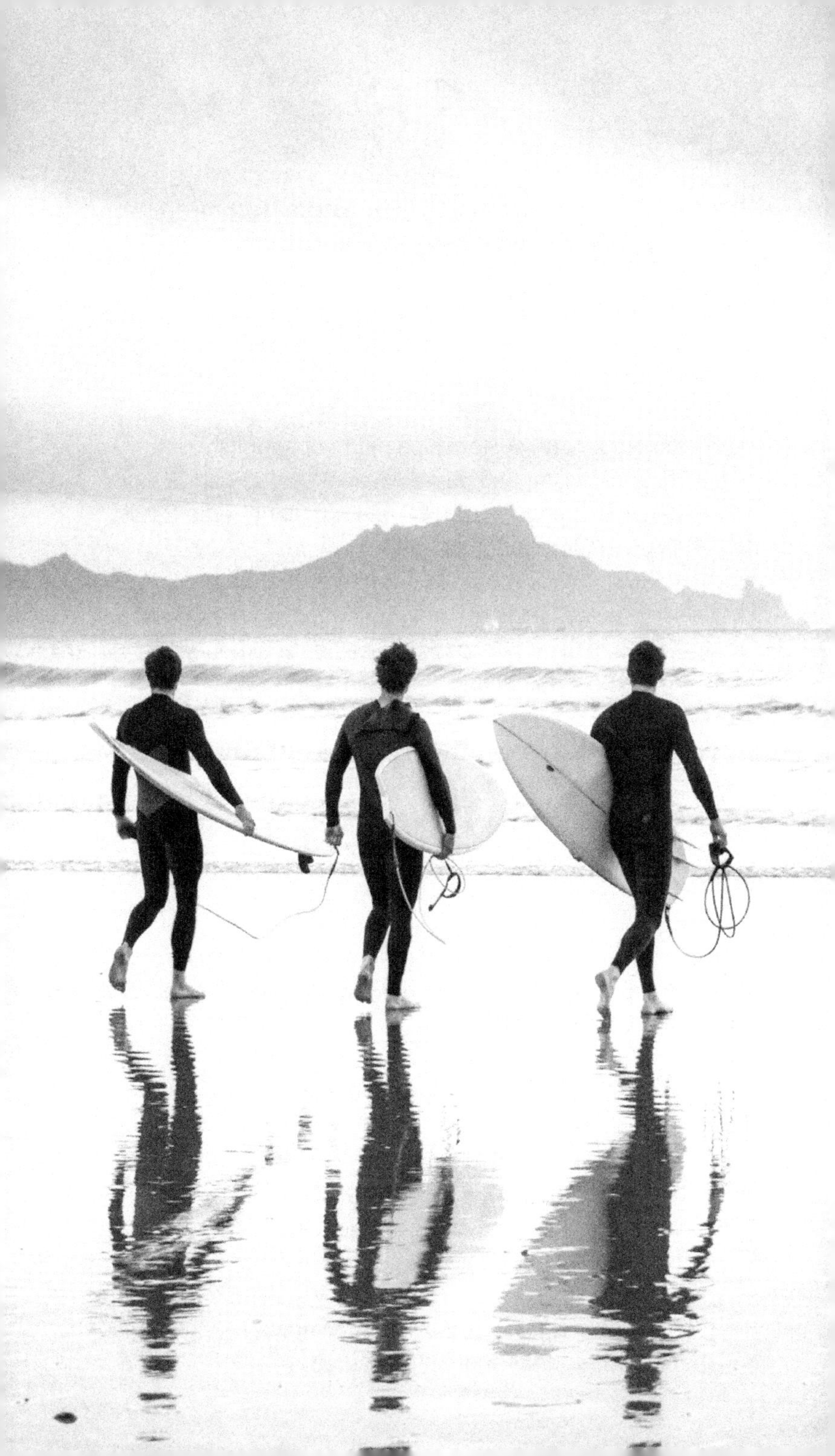

16

Places where the connection with nature becomes rawer, wilder, and sometimes even more dangerous.

In Galicia, for example, there is a community of surfers willing to take on one of the harshest and most rugged landscapes in Western Europe.

In this region of northwestern Spain, famous for its rocky coastline, sharp cliffs, and unpredictable weather, surfers ride waves between steep rock walls, with hurricane-force winds, and at times, under thunderstorms.

These extreme sessions are not random occurrences but rather the result of an almost poetic desire to experience surfing in its most primal and courageous form.

Riding the Galician sea when the skies open and electricity charges the air may seem insane, and it certainly is from a risk perspective, but it is also an expression of the visceral bond that some surfers maintain with the ocean, even when it turns hostile.

The most well-known wave in this context is A Lanzada, but there are many other breaks hidden among the estuaries and cliffs of the Costa da Morte.

The surfers who venture out under thunderstorms are usually experienced locals who know every crack of the rocky seabed and can read the ocean with precision, although the real threat of a lightning strike in open water turns these sessions into acts of resistance and devotion rather than simple athletic training.

For them, surfing under the roar of thunder is a mystical experience, where fear and beauty merge.

Far from Galicia, on the volcanic and glacial coasts of Iceland, another form of radical surfing takes place, this time under the dancing lights of the Northern Lights.

There, surfers with an adventurous spirit ride icy waves in an environment that feels closer to another planet than to a traditional beach.

To withstand the extreme water temperatures, which can drop to 2°C or lower in winter, surfers must wear special suits with internal heating systems, incorporating thermal layers, battery-powered heated panels, and high-tech gloves and booties.

On top of that, there's the challenge of logistics: access via ice-covered roads, physical preparation to surf with limited mobility, and a psychological tolerance to cold that pushes the boundaries of the human body.

Surfing under the Northern Lights is not just a physical challenge: it is a unique sensory experience.

The green and violet lights moving across the night sky transform every wave into a vision from another world.

Icelandic beaches such as Thorli, the Reykjanes Peninsula, and certain secret spots near the Westman Islands have become dream destinations for adventure surfers, photographers, and documentary filmmakers.

It's not about big or perfect waves, but about waves accompanied by one of the most mesmerizing natural spectacles on the planet.

Those who have surfed under the Northern Lights speak of an absolute connection with the universe, a kind of moving meditation where the body fights against the cold while the mind surrenders to the beauty.

At the other end of the spectrum, far from the wild chaos of Galicia or the frozen beauty of Iceland, Japan has created its own approach to controlled surfing: artificial beaches with waves designed exclusively for surfing practice.

In a country where natural space is scarce and technological innovation is part of the cultural DNA, surfing has adapted to urban and controlled environments with a unique level of precision.

There are complexes like Shizunami Surf Stadium, where mechanical waves replicate real ocean conditions, with sections adaptable for beginners or high-level surfers.

The waves can be calibrated in size, speed, shape, and frequency, allowing repetitive and efficient practice that, in the ocean, would depend on chance.

These spaces not only serve to train professional athletes but also to promote surfing as an Olympic discipline (remember that Japan hosted the Tokyo 2020 Olympics, where surfing debuted as an Olympic sport).

Artificial waves allow surfers to perform dozens of maneuvers in less than an hour, something impossible in a natural ocean setting, and also allow for training at night, indoors, or even in the rain, opening a new dimension of surfing as an urban, accessible, and technologically advanced experience.

17

Gabriel Medina is one of the most emblematic figures in contemporary Brazilian sports and one of the most successful and charismatic surfers in the history of professional surfing.

Born on December 22, 1993, in Maresias, a small coastal district in the municipality of São Sebastião, in the state of São Paulo, Medina grew up in a humble family deeply connected to the sea.

From a very young age, he showed extraordinary talent for surfing, standing out for his balance, intuition, and technical aggressiveness even in complex conditions.

His mother, Simone, and his stepfather, Charles Rodrigues, played a fundamental role in his career, supporting him from his first local competitions to becoming an international phenomenon.

Medina burst into the elite of world surfing with unusual force.

In 2011, at just 17 years old, he joined the Championship Tour of the World Surf League (WSL), the most important circuit in the world.

In his first year, he already secured surprising victories at high-level events like Hossegor (France) and San Francisco, showcasing an acrobatic and competitive ability that even challenged veteran champions.

But his definitive breakthrough came in 2014, when he became the first Brazilian to win the world surfing title, defeating legends like Kelly Slater, Mick Fanning, and Joel Parkinson.

This victory was not just a personal achievement: it marked a before and after in the history of Brazilian surfing.

Until then, professional surfing had been dominated by Australians, Americans, and a few Hawaiians.

Medina's arrival at the top of the world rankings represented a shake-up in the geography of competitive surfing.

Brazil, which had traditionally been marginalized or underestimated in the sport, emerged with a new generation called the "Brazilian Storm," composed of surfers like Italo Ferreira, Filipe Toledo, Adriano de Souza, and Medina himself, who began winning international events regularly.

Medina quickly became the symbol of this revolution.

His impact was so profound that, after winning his first world championship, he was received by crowds at São Paulo's international airport as if he were a football idol.

Thousands of people awaited him with flags, chants, drums, and banners.

In his hometown, a caravan was organized that paralyzed traffic for hours.

He was also officially received by sitting Brazilian presidents and honored by sports, educational, and social institutions.

He was awarded medals of honor, appointed as an ambassador for Brazilian sports, and there were even proposals to name public spaces after him in recognition of his contribution to national pride.

Medina is not just a technical champion: he is also a style icon.

He is known for his ability to execute aerial maneuvers with extraordinary height and fluidity, for his tactical discipline in challenging waves, and for his mastery both in small surf and heavy barrels.

He has won championships in places as diverse as Tahiti, France, Australia, Portugal, and Hawaii, and has shown remarkable consistency in the world rankings.

In addition to his title in 2014, he repeated the feat in 2018 and again in 2021, solidifying himself as a three-time world champion, placing him among the greatest of all time.

Outside the water, Medina has built a strong personal brand.

He has millions of followers on social media, has starred in advertising campaigns for major brands like Rip Curl, Oi, Adidas, and Jeep, and has founded his own training institute for young surfers, the Gabriel Medina Institute, where he offers technical, psychological, nutritional, and logistical support to new Brazilian surf talents.

This center not only aims to train champions but also to shape citizens who are conscious of the ocean, the environment, and the effort required to achieve their goals.

Throughout his career, he has also experienced controversial moments: disputes with coaches, criticism of his reactions during competitions, and media episodes related to his personal life.

But far from weakening his image, these moments have helped cement him as a complex and human figure, with a strong character, overwhelming ambition, and unbreakable determination.

His relationship with other Brazilian surfers has at times been competitive, but it has also been marked by camaraderie and the collective sense of mission that characterizes the Brazilian Storm.

Among the most striking curiosities of his career is that Medina was the first professional surfer to receive massive coverage on non-sports Brazilian news outlets, and he has been compared to national sports legends like Ayrton Senna, Pelé, and Gustavo Kuerten due to his ability to inspire new generations.

He has also expressed his desire to represent the country in environmental causes and has supported campaigns for beach cleanups, ocean preservation, and youth education in coastal communities.

18

In the world of surfing, where the usual goal is to find the perfect wave near the coast, there are stories that completely break this paradigm and take the concept of "riding a board" to the limits of ocean exploration and human endurance.

Over the years, some surfers and extreme adventurers have decided to cross entire oceans not in traditional vessels, but on modified surfboards, many inspired by the design of stand-up paddle boards (SUP), but adapted with navigation elements such as sails, cabins, watertight compartments, and satellite orientation systems.

These journeys are not just athletic feats but also odysseys of survival, planning, and mental resilience.

The most iconic and well-documented case is that of South African Chris Bertish, who in 2017 became the first person to cross the Atlantic Ocean completely alone, paddling upright on a modified paddleboard.

Bertish departed from the city of Agadir, Morocco, on December 6, 2016, and arrived at the island of Antigua in the Caribbean on March 9, 2017, after traveling more than 7,500 kilometers in 93 days.

The board he used, specifically designed for this expedition, was a hybrid between a SUP and a lightweight vessel: it was nearly 6 meters long, had a small sealed cabin where he slept, stored freeze-dried food and electronic equipment, included solar panels to charge batteries, a desalination system to produce drinking water, and satellite communication devices.

The challenge was immense, as Bertish faced storms, waves

over six meters high, desperate calms, technical problems, physical exhaustion, and extreme isolation.

He slept in short intervals, setting alarms every 45 minutes to check the wind direction and current.

He lost more than 12 kilograms, suffered cuts, inflammations, and burns from the sun and salt, and yet he never stopped paddling.

His journey was not just a personal achievement: he also raised over $400,000 for social causes in South Africa, especially focused on children's health and access to education.

Upon arriving in Antigua, he was welcomed as a hero, not only for accomplishing something never attempted before but for doing so with a philosophy of perseverance, altruism, and respect for the ocean.

Before Bertish, there had already been transoceanic expeditions on adapted boards, although none under such pure stand-up paddle conditions.

In 2007, surfer and explorer Jamie Mitchell, also a specialist in long-distance paddling, had crossed long stretches of the Pacific on traditional paddleboards in relay teams, and others like Antonio de la Rosa —a Spanish adventurer— crossed the Atlantic in 2019, also paddling upright on a vessel similar to a giant board, though more robust than Bertish's.

De la Rosa covered more than 4,700 kilometers in 76 days, departing from St. John's, Newfoundland (Canada), and arriving on the northern coast of Spain.

His board included a solar power system, GPS, manual desalination device, and climate sensors, and his purpose was to raise awareness about climate change and the impact of waste on the ocean.

All these cases share the fact that the protagonists were not seeking speed or spectacle, but rather to experience the sea in its purest form, to face it without a motor, without company, without external assistance, relying only on their bodies, their minds, and a board as the bridge between them and the abyss of the ocean.

These journeys have been compared to the great nautical epics of history, only in this case not aboard ships or sailboats, but on minimal vessels, where each wave, each gust of wind, and each solitary day represents a physical and spiritual challenge.

The phenomenon has grown, and nowadays there are alternative records and extreme challenges based on using SUP or hybrid boards to cross not only seas but also rivers, canals, and giant lakes.

There are even endurance events where surfers must paddle for more than 24 hours non-stop, or connect archipelagos such as the Canary Islands or those in the South Pacific.

Some undertake these feats as personal challenges, others as environmental protests, and some as part of scientific expeditions to monitor microplastics or changes in surface ocean temperatures.

Technological evolution has also allowed these boards to include geolocation systems, satellite communication, autopilots, and even small self-stabilization systems.

19

Surfing, more than just a sport, is a deeply spiritual and symbolic way of life for millions of people around the world.

For many surfers, the ocean is not just a place to practice; it is a true temple, a sacred space where they connect with nature, with themselves, and with a community that shares the same codes, passions, and silences.

That is why it is not surprising that, when the time comes to say goodbye, the ocean becomes the chosen place to honor those who lived with surfing as an essential part of their identity.

Funeral ceremonies at sea, many of them deeply emotional and visually striking, have become an unofficial but widespread tradition within global surf culture.

One of the most well-known rituals is scattering a loved one's ashes inside the barrel of a wave, as if it were their final great ride, a symbolic farewell where the deceased literally merges with the energy of the sea.

In this act, family and friends paddle out together and wait for the precise moment when a wave forms its barrel — that perfect hollow every surfer dreams of inhabiting — to release the ashes, letting them disperse at the very heart of that explosion of force, foam, and light.

For those who witness it, it feels as if the person crosses over by riding one last glorious wave, returning to the ocean from which they came, without fear or pain.

Full funerals held at sea have also been documented, where a surfboard is used as a ceremonial coffin, specially modified to carry the ashes or, in some cases, a symbolic vessel.

These ceremonies take place in calm waters, usually at sunrise or sunset, and may include songs, collective silences, applause, prayers, and the traditional paddle-out, where surfers form a circle on their boards in the water.

Once gathered in a circle, each person often shares a few words, tosses flowers into the center, or even releases a white dove.

Afterward, they slap the water with their hands and palms in a farewell gesture that combines sadness and celebration.

These ocean funerals have not only been carried out privately or spontaneously.

In places like California, Hawaii, Australia, Portugal, and Brazil, large-scale events have been organized to honor legendary surfers or beloved community members.

In 2010, for example, an ocean farewell was held for Andy Irons, one of the most beloved champions in professional surfing, at Hanalei Bay (Kauai, Hawaii), where hundreds of surfers gathered in the water to form one of the largest paddle-outs ever seen, surrounded by flowers, Hawaiian chants, and tears.

Even religious elements have been woven into surfing in these contexts.

Christian masses have been celebrated on surfboards in the middle of the ocean, especially in countries like Brazil, where the fusion between religion and coastal culture is very strong.

In some of these ceremonies, a priest stands on a longboard alongside the congregation, reading Bible passages from the water, blessing those present, and consecrating communion in a symbolically powerful way.

These masses at sea aim to express that God is everywhere, even among the waves, and that faith can be practiced wherever one feels most connected to the divine.

Often, these ceremonies coincide with the anniversary of a deceased surfer and serve as rites of remembrance and community healing.

Beyond the religious or ceremonial aspects, what unites all these rituals is the vision of the sea as a place of passage, origin, and return.

For surfers, dying is not simply disappearing, but returning to the ocean that formed them, sustained them, challenged them, and gave them meaning.

It is about ceasing to paddle on the surface and merging with the liquid energy of something greater.

That's why scattering ashes into a wave, saying goodbye on a surfboard, or receiving a mass while floating in the ocean are not oddities or extravagant acts, but profound gestures that celebrate life from the sea, with the sea, and for the sea.

This type of tribute is also growing among non-surfers, inspired by the poetry of these farewells.

There are companies now that organize surf-style funeral ceremonies for anyone who wishes to be honored at sea, with custom boards, biodegradable floating flowers, live music, and the participation of friends and family, all with a respectful and ecological spirit.

It is a way of saying goodbye with freedom, beauty, and fluidity, allowing the body, or at least its memory, to become part of the waves.

Ultimately, these practices reveal just how much surfing is not just a sport, but a way of understanding existence.

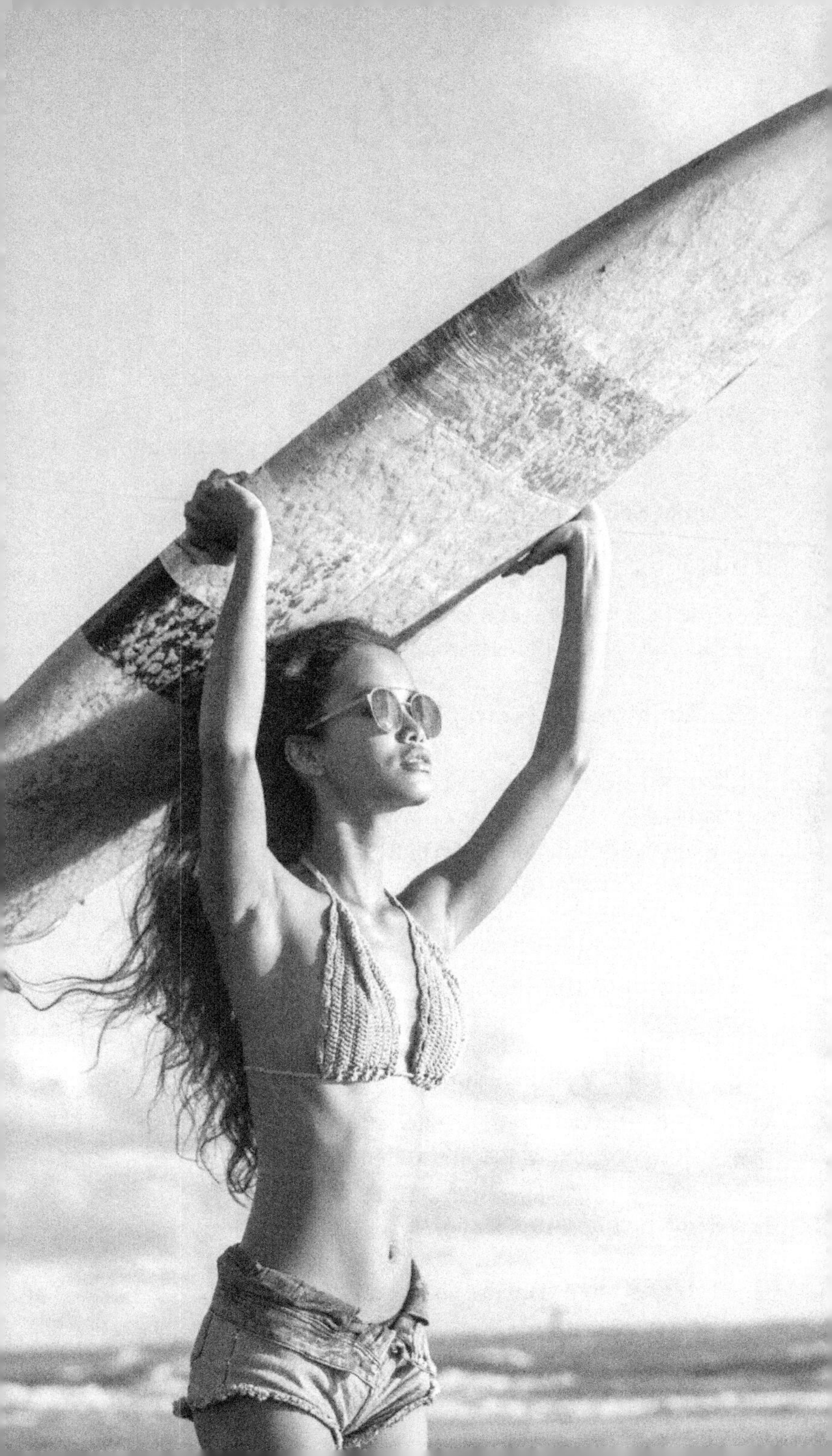

20

Famous Quotes.

1. Kelly Slater (USA)

- "The best surfer is the one having the most fun."
- "There is no secret, just consistency and love for what you do."
- "The ocean never lies; it always puts you in your place."

2. Duke Kahanamoku (Hawaii)

- "Out of the water, I am nothing."
- "The best way to surf a wave is to respect it."
- "Spread aloha wherever you go."

3. Gabriel Medina (Brazil)

- "Surfing gave me everything, even when I thought I had lost it."
- "Every wave is an opportunity to start over."
- "I don't compete against others; I compete against my own limits."

4. Andy Irons (Hawaii)

- "The ocean saved my life many times... and took it away just as often."
- "There is no victory without darkness."
- "When I'm in the water, I don't think, I just am."

5. Mick Fanning (Australia)

- "I learned more from the shark than from my titles."
- "Calmness is your best weapon in the middle of the storm."
- "Sometimes losing teaches you how to truly win."

6. Tom Curren (USA)

- "Surfing is music in motion."
- "I don't need words when I have waves."
- "Style is stronger than strength."

7. Laird Hamilton (USA)

- "There's no purer adrenaline than looking a giant wave in the eye."
- "Living without fear isn't living, it's hiding."
- "Discipline creates the freedom to surf any wave."

8. Stephanie Gilmore (Australia)

- "Surfing has no gender, only passion."
- "A good wave changes your day, a great wave changes your life."
- "Elegance is surfing without making noise."

9. Layne Beachley (Australia)

- "I didn't come to be the best woman surfer. I came to be the best, period."
- "Fear tests you. Courage defines you."
- "The ocean gives you answers that the land doesn't have."

10. Carissa Moore (USA)

- "There are no small waves if the heart is big."
- "My best surfing comes when I stop trying to win."
- "Being a champion isn't the end; it's the beginning of another story."

11. Bethany Hamilton (USA)

- "My passion is bigger than my fears."
- "I don't need two arms to hug a wave."
- "The ocean gave me back what life took from me."

12. Mark Richards (Australia)

- "Being a four-time champion doesn't feel better than a single perfect barrel."
- "The board is your brush. The sea, your canvas."
- "Surfing is an endless conversation with water."

13. Joel Parkinson (Australia)

- "Patience makes the surfer."
- "The best waves come when you stop searching for them."
- "The ocean doesn't reward haste, it rewards reading."

14. Julian Wilson (Australia)

- "Surfing is risk, but also art."
- "My mind surfs before my body does."
- "Every wave holds a secret; you just have to learn to listen."

15. Filipe Toledo (Brazil)

- "If you can fly on a wave, you can fly in life."
- "Every maneuver is a leap of faith."
- "Air becomes part of the ocean when you surf it right."

16. Italo Ferreira (Brazil)

- "The favela can also produce world champions."
- "I don't surf for trophies; I surf because I was born to."
- "The ocean doesn't discriminate, it only challenges."

17. Chris Bertish (South Africa)

- "Crossing the Atlantic standing wasn't madness, it was purpose."
- "When you paddle for days, you learn who you are."
- "Big waves are like big dreams: they scare you, but they transform you."

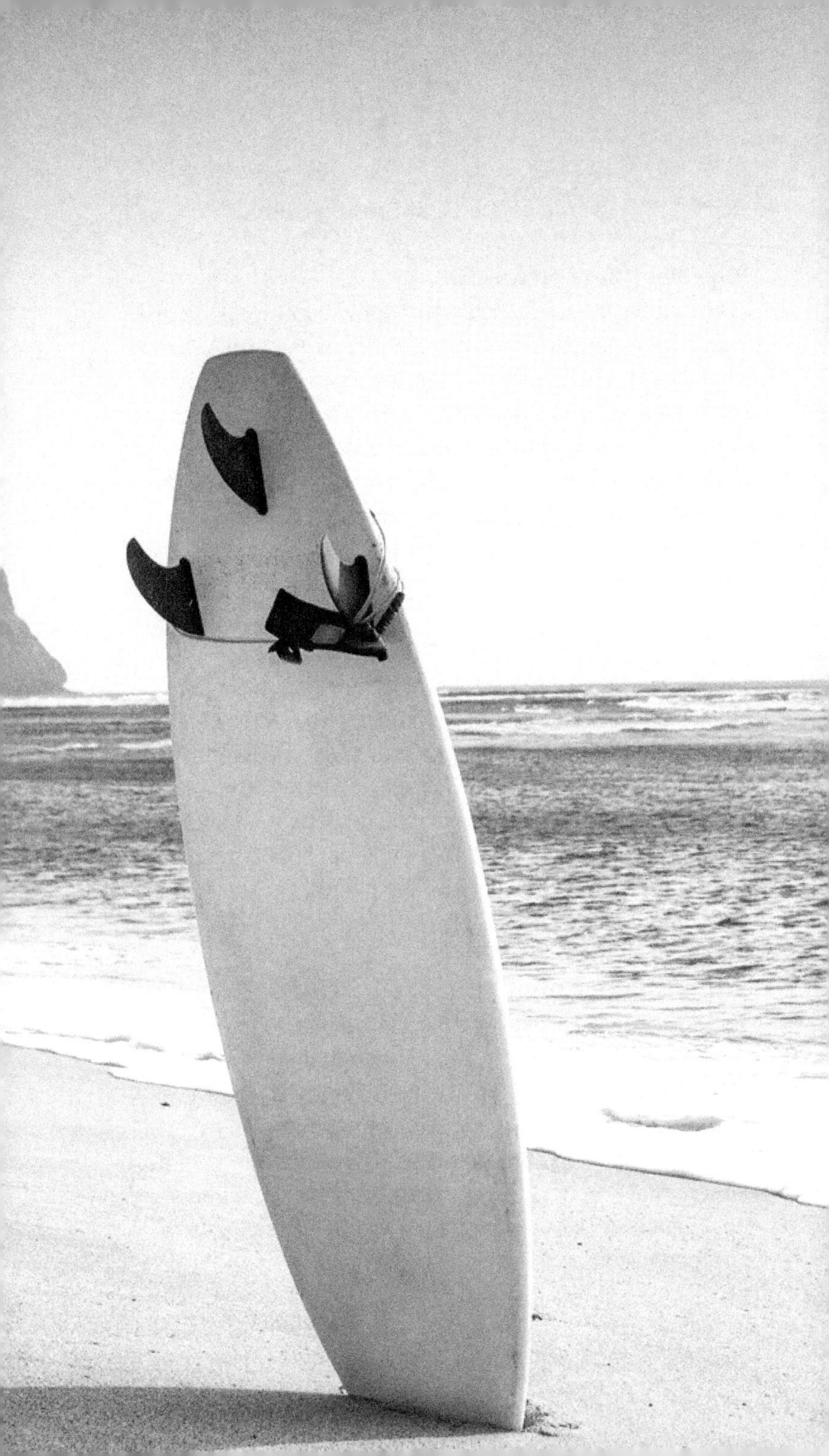

21

Some of the Best Surfing Spots.

- Pipeline (Oahu, Hawaii, USA):
It is probably the most iconic surf spot in the world. Its fame comes from the perfection and danger of its barrels, which break over a very sharp and shallow reef. It's an extremely technical and brutal wave, where mistakes are paid for with serious injuries. Legends like Kelly Slater, Andy Irons, and John John Florence have made their mark here. Pipeline is the traditional venue for the Pipe Masters, one of the most legendary events of the Championship Tour, and it is considered the spiritual mecca of high-risk surfing.

- Teahupo'o (Tahiti, French Polynesia)
Known as the most feared wave in the world. Its lip is so thick it looks like a curtain of concrete falling from the sky. It breaks almost dry over sharp coral and has caused numerous severe injuries among elite surfers. Laird Hamilton, Nathan Florence, and Maya Gabeira have bravely faced it. Its tubular perfection is almost unreal, and its danger makes it one of the most sacred and respected spots on the planet, chosen to host the surfing event for Paris 2024 Olympics.

- Nazaré (Portugal)
Home to the largest waves ever surfed thanks to its 5,000-meter-deep underwater canyon that channels oceanic energy toward the shore. Garrett McNamara made history here by surfing a wave estimated to be over 30 meters. António Laureano and Maya Gabeira have also set records here. It is the epicenter of big wave surfing and a place where every session puts lives at risk. Nazaré is pure oceanic adrenaline.

- Jaws (Pe'ahi, Maui, Hawaii)
It is synonymous with power. Its waves can exceed 20 meters

and move at breakneck speeds, making tow-in surfing essential. Kai Lenny, Mark Visser, and Shane Dorian have bravely and skillfully challenged its liquid walls. The violence with which it breaks and the roar it emits before breaking make it one of the most impressive waves on the planet. On big days, Jaws is a spectacle of nature and human courage.

- Snapper Rocks (Gold Coast, Australia)
It offers one of the most perfect and fastest right-handers in the world. It's a wave that seems designed for modern surfing: long, with maneuverable sections, ideal for aerials and powerful turns. Surfers like Mick Fanning, Joel Parkinson, and Stephanie Gilmore grew up mastering this wave, elevating its international status. Beyond its quality, it is the heart of Australian surf culture, with a unique competitive and technical spirit.

- Jeffreys Bay (South Africa)
Known as J-Bay, it's a kilometer-long right-hander with multiple sections where speed and style are rewarded. Kelly Slater, Jordy Smith, and Mick Fanning have surfed it masterfully, and it's famous for the barrels it offers in its most critical section: Supertubes. It's also known for the shark attack on Fanning during a live event in 2015. The natural beauty of its surroundings and the consistency of its waves make it one of the jewels of world surfing.

- Uluwatu (Bali, Indonesia)
It is one of the most legendary surf spots in Southeast Asia and one of the first reef breaks discovered by Western surfers in the 1970s. It has multiple peaks that break at different tides and offer long barrels. Rob Machado and Gerry Lopez have surfed its waves during historic moments. It's a place that combines Balinese mystique with the technical challenge of reef surfing, making it a must-visit destination for experienced surfers.

- Trestles (California, USA)
Located in San Clemente, it offers clean waves with a stone

and sand bottom, ideal for modern maneuvers. Kelly Slater, Tom Curren, and Carissa Moore have used it as a testing ground for innovating style and technique. It's one of the professionals' favorite training spots and a host for WSL events. Its proximity to urban centers and the quality of its waves have made it the laboratory of progressive surfing.

- Hossegor (France)
It's the best beach break in Europe, famous for its powerful barrels breaking over sandbanks. In autumn, when the big Atlantic swells arrive, it transforms into a tubular battleground comparable to Pipeline. Gabriel Medina, Jeremy Flores, and Mick Fanning have all shined here during multiple tour stops. It's a place where the ocean's power meets the energy of the European crowd.

- Cloudbreak (Tavarua, Fiji)
It's a powerful left-hand wave breaking over a reef that can deliver perfect barrels up to 5 meters or more. Its scenic beauty contrasts with its technical difficulty. Surfers like Kelly Slater, Gabriel Medina, and Bethany Hamilton have delivered legendary performances here. It's considered one of the most consistent and dangerous waves in the South Pacific, with fast and demanding sections.

- Skeleton Bay (Namibia)
It offers one of the longest and most perfect waves in the world: a left that can last over a minute in a continuous barrel. Koa Smith and Benji Brand have had epic sessions here, documenting rides that seem endless. It's an extremely remote and hard-to-predict spot, but when it breaks under ideal conditions, it's a miracle of nature. Discovered by satellite in 2008, it revolutionized the understanding of wave length in surfing.

- Bells Beach (Victoria, Australia)
It's a powerful wave that breaks over a rocky bottom and demands precision in every turn. It hosts the Rip Curl Pro, the oldest surfing competition in the world. Surfers like Mick

Fanning, Stephanie Gilmore, and Kelly Slater have made history here. Its golden bell trophy is one of the most coveted prizes in professional surfing. Bells represents tradition, power, and deep respect for the history of Australian surfing.

- Punta de Lobos (Chile)

It's the big wave paradise of South America. Its long, thick left-handers break forcefully over a rocky bottom. Ramón Navarro has made this place his home and battlefield. On big days, the waves exceed 8 meters. Additionally, it's a natural sanctuary and a symbol of coastal conservation. Its dramatic landscape and wild energy make it a magical place.

- Mundaka (Basque Country, Spain)

It's famous for having the best left-hand wave in continental Europe. It breaks at the mouth of a river and offers long, fast, and technically challenging barrels. Aritz Aranburu and Dane Reynolds have stood out here. Although it experiences variable conditions, when it aligns properly, it's a world-class wave. Its blend of Basque culture, green landscapes, and quality surf makes it unique.

- Shonan and Chiba (Japan)

They are the hearts of Japanese surfing. Chiba hosted the Olympic surfing event in 2020 and offers clean, consistent waves. Surfers like Kanoa Igarashi and Hiroto Ohhara often train and compete here. Japanese surf culture combines respect, technique, and discipline. The waves may not be massive, but their consistency and the infrastructure make these beaches central hubs of Asian surfing.

22

Italo Ferreira is one of the most explosive, charismatic, and resilient surfers in modern surf history, and his name was forever etched into global sports history when he became the first Olympic surfing champion at the Tokyo 2020 Games, held in 2021 due to the pandemic.

Born on May 6, 1994, in Baía Formosa, a small fishing village in the state of Rio Grande do Norte, northeastern Brazil, Italo grew up in humble conditions, with a childhood marked by hard work, family efforts, and a deep connection to the sea.

His first surfboard wasn't a professional one: it was built by his father, assembled from pieces of foam and improvised wood.

Italo learned to surf standing on the lids of the ice coolers his family used to sell fish.

From a young age, he showed boundless energy and an overwhelming passion for the waves.

His style was aggressive, unpredictable, and full of aerials, which caught the attention of legendary talent scout Luiz "Pinga" Campos, who decided to support him in his first trips to junior championships.

In 2011, he began competing in national tournaments, and in 2014 he was invited to participate in the Qualifying Series, where he quickly proved his talent was different.

A year later, in 2015, he entered the World Surf League (WSL) Championship Tour (CT) and was named Rookie of the Year thanks to his consistency and electrifying approach to every wave.

From there, his rise was unstoppable.

In 2019, after a season of intense competition with Gabriel Medina and Kolohe Andino, Italo won his first world title in the CT Grand Final at Pipeline, Hawaii, becoming the world surfing champion.

He achieved this by combining his explosive power with a defiant attitude that broke away from the traditional calmness of the classic surfer.

His aerial maneuvers, especially his full rotations and backflips, made him one of the most spectacular surfers on the circuit.

But it was in 2021 that he reached the peak of his global significance by becoming the first surfer in history to win an Olympic gold medal, during surfing's debut as an Olympic discipline.

The event took place at Tsurigasaki Beach in Chiba, Japan.

Ferreira not only won gold: he did so in epic fashion, breaking his board on the first wave of the final against Japan's Kanoa Igarashi and having to switch boards mid-competition.

Despite that setback, he recovered with almost supernatural energy and delivered a dominating performance, landing radical maneuvers that the judges rewarded with very high scores.

At the end, he burst into tears, fell to his knees in the sand, and embraced the Brazilian flag.

His victory was celebrated across the country as a historic achievement, and his image became a symbol of perseverance and national pride.

Outside the water, Italo is a magnetic figure.

He has always remained close to his roots, constantly

returning to Baía Formosa to connect with the community and organize projects for inclusion, training, and support for underprivileged children.

He maintains an active, joyful, and intensely energetic lifestyle.

He is passionate about physical training, music, and travel, and he has earned the respect of the surfing circuit not only for his performance but also for his tireless attitude, humility, and constant gratitude.

Among his most striking traits is his way of celebrating: on several occasions, he has been seen screaming to the sky, sprinting like lightning across the sand, or doing backflips.

He is an emotional athlete who channels his intensity into every heat he surfs.

He is also deeply religious and has credited his victories to his faith in God, often repeating phrases like "Deus é fiel" ("God is faithful") at the end of each competition.

23

Nude surfing competitions, though unconventional and outside the professional circuit, do exist and hold a peculiar place within surf culture, especially in countries like Australia, where the relationship with the body, freedom, and nature is lived openly, playfully, and without inhibition.

These competitions are not part of the official World Surf League calendar nor focused on high performance; rather, they are alternative, symbolic events filled with humor and a community spirit, celebrating surfing as a pure act of connection between humans and the ocean, without filters, brands, fabric, or egos.

In Australia, where nude beaches are legal along certain stretches of coastline and beach culture runs deep, several editions of what are known as "nudie surf competitions" or informal nude surf gatherings have been organized, typically during coastal community events, beach festivals, or themed celebrations like World Naked Surfing Day, an unofficial day promoted by naturist groups and free-spirited surfers aiming to destigmatize the body and reclaim a more primal surfing experience, closer to its Polynesian roots.

One of the best-known places for such activities is Byron Bay in New South Wales, a capital of alternative surf culture and Australian counterculture.

There, at beaches like Tyagarah or Belongil, it's common during specific festivities or hot summer days to see small tournaments or collective nude surfing sessions take place.

These sessions usually have more relaxed rules: there are no official judges, scores are symbolic, and what is rewarded is charisma, style, humor, connection with the wave, and above all, boldness.

In many cases, surfers use accessories like hats, body paint, or partial costumes, always under the motto of total freedom and zero shame.

These competitions also carry a message of protest: they criticize the excessive commercialization of modern surfing, where brands, sponsors, and commercial aesthetics have often replaced the rebellious, free, and creative spirit with which the discipline was born.

By surfing naked, participants make a statement: you don't need lycra or logos to feel the wave, just a willing body and a board floating over the energy of the sea.

Additionally, these activities are often associated with values of inclusion, respect for body diversity, self-acceptance, and mental health.

Some organizers argue that surfing naked helps overcome body insecurities, generates a sense of vulnerability that strengthens self-esteem, and promotes a more honest relationship with oneself.

In naturist communities, nude surfing is actually seen not as an eccentricity, but as a natural activity, where the skin makes direct contact with the breeze, the salt, and the board, enhancing sensations and emotions different from conventional surfing.

Regarding safety, certain precautions are, of course, taken: days with very large waves or overly technical conditions are avoided, participation is limited to adults, and rules of mutual respect and appropriate behavior are established.

The boards are sometimes adapted with special waxes to prevent slipping, and the relaxed, festive atmosphere is prioritized over any sense of competitiveness.

Outside of Australia, similar events have also been recorded in places like California, New Zealand, South Africa, and some naturist beaches in France and Brazil, although less frequently.

There are even nude surfers who document their adventures on social media or in alternative documentaries, reclaiming surfing as a free practice, unbound by fashion or professional circuits.

24

There are blind surfers who defy all the physical and mental limits of the sport by facing the waves guided solely by the sounds of the ocean, the sensations in their bodies, and, in many cases, the verbal guidance of an assistant from the shore or in the water.

Far from being a rarity, adapted surfing for people with visual impairments has developed as a branch of inclusive surfing, where passion, trust, and intuition replace sight and become the true senses that dominate the board.

What these surfers achieve is profoundly impressive, not only from a technical standpoint but also from an emotional and human perspective: entering the sea without seeing what is coming, reading a wave through the vibration of the water, and maintaining balance with almost exclusively tactile and auditory references is a feat of extreme sensitivity.

These surfers perceive the proximity of a wave by the change in the sound produced by the breaking water: large waves generate a deeper, more enveloping roar, while smaller waves emit a lighter crackle.

They also feel how the pressure of the water against their legs changes and how their board responds to the movements of the ocean.

Some develop a kind of "sixth sense" that allows them to anticipate the behavior of the wave without the need to see it, by reading subtle cues in the energy of the surroundings.

Many use a guide or companion who gives them instructions from behind, shouting key words like "left," "right," "paddle," "stand up."

They even have assistants on jet skis or at the break line who use special sounds or whistles as signals.

In adaptive surfing championships organized by the International Surfing Association (ISA), there are specific categories for surfers with visual impairments, called VI-1 and VI-2, which distinguish between those who are completely blind and those who have some degree of functional vision.

In these competitions, surfers can rely on an assistant in the water who helps them position themselves in the right spot and gives them verbal signals when it's time to paddle or turn.

The process is so well coordinated that it looks like choreography, but it is actually the result of hours of training based on absolute trust.

One of the most inspiring cases is that of Brazilian surfer Derek Rabelo, who was born completely blind due to congenital glaucoma and yet learned to surf at the age of 17.

He became famous worldwide for his ability to surf big waves, even at Pipeline (Hawaii), one of the most dangerous surf spots on the planet.

Rabelo trains intensively in balance techniques, muscle memory, and spatial localization.

His story was documented in the film Beyond Sight, which portrayed his learning process, his fears, his repeated falls, and his transformation into a global example of perseverance and connection with the sea.

Derek not only surfs out of passion, but he also gives motivational talks and collaborates on projects to promote adaptive surfing in communities with disabilities.

Another leading figure is Matt Formston, an Australian who lost his sight due to a degenerative disease, and who not only surfs but also competes in professional tournaments of adaptive surfing, cycling, and other sports.

Formston states that his connection with the ocean has deepened since he lost his vision, as he relies entirely on his focus, senses, and trust to ride a wave.

He has represented Australia in adaptive surfing world championships and has won multiple titles.

Training for a blind surfer involves working on hearing, balance (especially through exercises on unstable surfaces), reaction to sounds, and communication with their guide.

The surfboard can also be customized with textures that help identify the position where they should be placed or with raised details on the wax.

Technology has also started to play an important role, with the development of waterproof headphones that allow direct transmission of commands from the shore, or even sensors that vibrate when detecting an approaching wave.

25

Superstitions and rituals.

1. Kelly Slater
He avoids surfing with brightly colored shirts in competition.
He believes that black and white help him stay focused.
He is also very meticulous about the order of his belongings before each heat and practices disciplined meditation.

2. Duke Kahanamoku
The legendary father of modern surfing would say a prayer to the ocean before every session. According to testimonies, he had a deep ritual respect for the sea and never entered the water without making a traditional Hawaiian gesture or greeting.

3. Gabriel Medina
He always makes the sign of the cross before paddling toward his first competitive wave. He also wears a silver cross necklace as a good luck charm and believes he should only take it off once he's in the water.

4. Andy Irons
He believed that wearing a red shirt gave him power, and many of his victories were while wearing that color. He also avoided surfing after eating fish, following a superstition passed down by a Hawaiian fisherman.

5. Mick Fanning
Since his famous encounter with a shark, he always carries a shark tooth necklace for protection. He has a ritual of taking three deep breaths right before his heat begins.

6. Tom Curren
He is deeply introspective. Before surfing, he isolates himself, walks alone along the

beach, and is believed not to allow anyone to touch his board on competition day, as part of a personal energetic connection.

7. Laird Hamilton
His preparation is almost shamanic. He performs ice immersions and meditation before entering big water. He believes that the cold purifies his energy and spiritually "resets" him to face giant waves.

8. Stephanie Gilmore
She always touches the water three times before entering and never competes without her favorite wax, which must have a coconut scent. She also listens to the same playlist before each heat.

9. Layne Beachley
She practiced visualization with stones. She would choose a stone before her heat, hold it in her hand for a few seconds, and then throw it into the sea as a symbolic offering to the wave.

10. Carissa Moore
She carries a sticker on her board with a mantra handwritten by her mother. She never rides any competition board without that message and touches it with her fingers before paddling out.

11. Bethany Hamilton
After her accident, Bethany developed a ritual of giving thanks to the sea every time she enters the water. She says a small prayer and fully submerges herself for a few seconds as a sign of respect and rebirth.

12. Mark Richards
He avoided changing boards in the middle of a championship, even if it was damaged. He believed that once a board won a heat, it had to be used until the end of the event.

13. Joel Parkinson
He would always draw a small figure in the sand with his toe before entering the sea. It was a kind of symbolic signature, a private ritual he had repeated since his teenage years.

14. Julian Wilson
He always uses the same color for the rear grip on his competition boards. When his mother was diagnosed with cancer, he started using pink and turned it into a symbol of strength. Since then, he has never changed it.

15. Filipe Toledo
He never enters the water without giving his board three slaps. He says it's a way to "wake it up" before each session. He also always listens to the same song right before heading into the sea.

16. Italo Ferreira
He is extremely superstitious about his equipment. He doesn't allow anyone to touch his leash or board, and he always starts the engine of his jet ski with the same hand when surfing big waves. Additionally, he prays out loud before each heat.

17. Chris Bertish
The adventurer who crossed the Atlantic on a SUP carried a small volcanic stone from Hawaii tied to his wrist as a protective talisman. He also had the habit of shouting a motivational phrase to the ocean at the start of each day in open water.

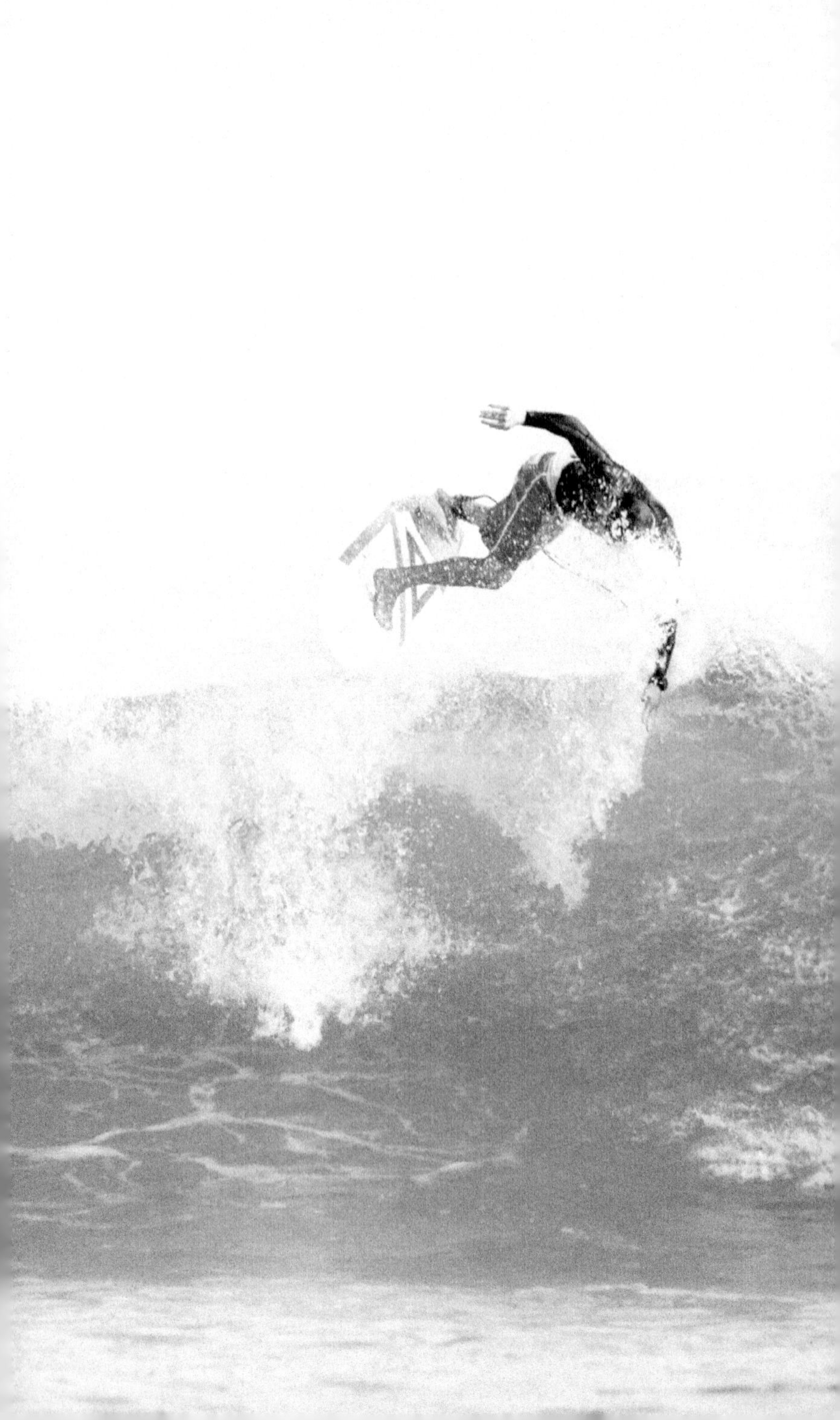

26

In Mexico, there is a wave called "La Ticla," located on the coast of the state of Michoacán, which is not only recognized for its exceptional quality for surfing but also as a unique example of cultural resistance, community protection, and indigenous identity.

This break is found at the mouth of the Ostula River, on lands belonging to the indigenous Nahua community of Santa María Ostula, an original people who have defended their territory against external interests for generations and who have achieved something rare in the surfing world: preserving a world-class wave as a collective asset, under their own control, without allowing it to be commercially or massively exploited.

La Ticla is a powerful, consistent, and very long left-hand wave that breaks over a sandy bottom with a quality that, during the Pacific swell season between April and October, can rival world-famous surf spots.

Although it is not as media-covered as Puerto Escondido or other Mexican surf destinations, surfers who have had the chance to experience it in person agree that its shape is perfect for long maneuvers, controlled barrels, and technical sessions.

Its strongest point is its consistency, as it breaks almost year-round, with clean waves, favorable winds, and without the overcrowding that affects other beaches, but what truly makes La Ticla special is its history of community self-defense.

The community of Ostula has been at the forefront of a complex struggle against armed groups, drug trafficking, land invaders, hotel interests, and government structures that have tried to seize control of the area.

In 2009, after decades of conflict, the Nahuas of Ostula decided to reclaim their ancestral lands through direct action, founding the territorial recovery project called "La Encargatura de Xayakalan."

Since then, they have protected not only their fields, mountains, and rivers, but also the coast and the wave of La Ticla.

Access to the wave is managed directly by the community, which regulates tourism, controls development, and does not allow large private investments or constructions that could disrupt the environmental or cultural balance of the area.

Visitors must respect the community's internal rules, pay a community fee, and accept that they are entering an autonomous indigenous territory.

This vision of defense and care has allowed La Ticla to remain one of the few surfing sanctuaries where nature and indigenous culture coexist in harmony, and where surfing is a respectful, non-invasive activity.

In resistance events, marches, and gatherings of indigenous peoples, Ostula representatives have spoken of surfing as a tool for intercultural dialogue, as many surfers who arrive there with respect become allies of their struggle.

Community surfing initiatives have even emerged to teach Nahua youth how to surf, build their own boards, and find in the sea a way to channel identity, strength, and rootedness.

There are stories of local teenagers who learned to surf on donated or recycled boards and who now dream of representing their people in national tournaments, but always with a collective mindset.

On an ecological level, La Ticla has also been defended against extractivist projects, deforestation, and pollution.

The community has blocked roads, protested in front of authorities, and built its own surveillance network to prevent the entry of illegal machinery or individuals seeking to exploit natural resources without consent.

For the Nahuas of Ostula, the wave is not a sporting resource: it is a living manifestation of nature, a spirit of the land that is part of their worldview.

The fame of La Ticla has grown slowly but authentically.

Renowned surfers who have traveled all over the world recognize it as a hidden treasure, a gem that offers not only high-quality waves but also a profound cultural and spiritual experience.

In a world where many beaches have been transformed into resorts, La Ticla stands as a powerful reminder that surfing can exist without destruction, that it can flourish through autonomy and respect, and that there are waves that are not only surfed with technique, but also with awareness.

27

Seiichi Sano, a Japanese man born in 1933, became an iconic figure in the surfing world in 2023 when he was officially recognized by the Guinness World Records as the oldest active surfer on the planet, at 89 years old at the time of certification.

His story not only surprised the surfing community due to his exceptional physical longevity, but also served as a global inspiration by demonstrating that passion, curiosity, and the desire to learn have no expiration date, and that even at advanced ages, personal limits can be challenged and new adventures explored.

The most extraordinary thing about Seiichi Sano is that he started surfing at the age of 80, a time when most people tend to step away from impact sports or the sea.

Before entering the world of surfing, Sano worked for decades in Japan's corporate sector, serving as a manager at a systems construction company.

After retiring, he decided not to settle into a conventional retirement, but instead to use his time to challenge himself.

He had already climbed Mount Fuji, and after that experience, he sought another activity that would give him energy, freedom, and a connection with nature.

That's how he discovered surfing.

His first contact with the board happened at the beaches of Chigasaki, in Kanagawa Prefecture, a coastal area traditionally popular among Japanese surfers.

Driven by his restless spirit and the desire to stay physically and mentally active, Sano enrolled in private surfing lessons and began training under the guidance of young instructors who, in many cases, were more than six decades younger than him.

His progress was slow but steady.

He learned to read the sea, to maintain balance, to paddle with discipline, and, most importantly, to listen to his body without pushing it, respecting his own rhythms.

Despite his age, Sano surfs once a week, and he does so with the attitude of a teenager discovering the ocean for the first time.

He uses a longboard, ideal for small, gentle waves, which allows him to glide with stability.

He doesn't perform spectacular maneuvers or deep barrels, but he stands up, flows with the wave, and lets himself be carried by the ocean's energy with enviable serenity.

For him, surfing is not an athletic feat but an act of active meditation, a way of being present, of living the moment intensely, and of proving that the passage of time does not erase the desire to play with life.

What has most captured attention about his story is not just his age, but his philosophy of life.

In interviews, he has said that he is not interested in "living a long time," but in "living with intention, with purpose."

He believes that surfing connects him with a vital energy that rejuvenates him, keeps him alert, and forces him to move, to breathe deeply, to face fears, and to celebrate achievements, even small ones.

He has also mentioned that surfing has taught him to accept

failure without frustration, as many times he is unable to stand up on the board, but he never feels defeated, only motivated to try again.

Seiichi Sano has become a symbol of active aging, an example of how the body can remain functional and strong when physical activity is combined with mental and emotional motivation.

His case has been studied by doctors and trainers, who highlight his flexibility, balance, and cardiovascular condition as remarkable qualities for someone his age.

He attributes his well-being to a balanced diet, surfing, and not allowing himself to be trapped by the inertia of a sedentary lifestyle or routine.

In Japan, a country with one of the longest-living populations in the world, Sano's story has been especially meaningful.

In a society where retirement and aging are often experienced with resignation, Sano has shown that old age can also be a stage of discovery, of deep connection with nature, and of continuous learning.

Thanks to his achievement, he has become a popular figure, given talks, appeared on television programs, and inspired many older people to resume or start physical activities, especially those involving contact with water.

He does not seek fame, sponsors, or recognition: his only goal is to keep enjoying the sea, as after receiving the Guinness World Record, he humbly said that he is "still learning" and hopes to improve his technique.

For many young and veteran surfers, Sano represents the purest essence of surfing, the kind that is not measured by maneuvers or titles, but by the love for the wave, the connection with the sea, and the courage to dive into the water once more, regardless of age, doubts, or limitations.

28

There are beaches in various parts of the world where the waves glow with bioluminescence, an astonishing natural phenomenon that turns the ocean into an otherworldly visual spectacle, especially at night.

This glow occurs thanks to the presence of microscopic marine organisms—mainly dinoflagellates—that emit light when disturbed by the movement of the water.

When a wave breaks, when someone swims, or even when a surfboard is paddled, these organisms react by producing an electric blue glow, as if the sea were lighting up from within.

The result is a magical and surreal sight: waves that seem to have a life of their own, traced by streaks of light following the surfer's movements.

The phenomenon of marine bioluminescence is neither constant nor as predictable as the tides, as it depends on a combination of factors such as water temperature, nutrient concentration, salinity, the presence of algae, and ambient darkness.

However, there are certain places in the world where the conditions occur relatively often, turning these beaches into points of interest not only for scientists and photographers but also for surfers who wish to experience the thrill of riding waves that glow in the dark.

Among the most well-known locations for this phenomenon are Puerto Rico (particularly Mosquito Bay and Laguna Grande), the Maldives, San Diego and Laguna Beach in California, Jervis Bay in Australia, Manila in the Philippines, and Manzanillo Beach in Mexico.

In many of these places, night surfing under bioluminescence is not a regular practice or organized as a recurring event, due to the inherent risks of surfing at night (lack of visibility, currents, unseen obstacles), but there have been special occasions—either through individual initiative or visual projects—where professional surfers have entered the water to ride these glowing waves.

One of the most famous cases was the visual project carried out in 2011 by Australian surfer Mark Visser, known for challenging extreme conditions.

Visser surfed waves at Jaws, Hawaii, during the night, wearing a suit equipped with LED lights, which, although not in a natural bioluminescent setting, created similar images that later inspired real explorations of the phenomenon.

Later on, in places like Laguna Beach, local surfers and photographers like Tobias Raphael captured images of surfers tracing lines of light over the sea, creating a spectacular visual effect without artificial lighting, using only natural bioluminescence.

In the Maldives, surfers and travelers have reported spontaneous sessions at beaches like Vaadhoo Island, where the shores light up in blue as you walk or paddle over the water.

Although night surfing is not common for safety reasons, some have practiced bodyboarding or simply floated with their boards to watch how every movement generates a flash beneath their hands and feet.

In San Diego, local surfers have entered the water during bioluminescent swells, creating bluish trails of light that follow the outline of the wave and the surfer's body, an experience many have described as "surfing in a dream."

Bioluminescence has also been a source of artistic and

cinematic inspiration in the context of surfing.

In documentaries, short films, and advertising campaigns, this experience has been portrayed with special effects or real footage captured with high-sensitivity cameras, showing what it feels like to glide across a wave that lights up with every second.

For the surfers who have lived this experience—
though they are few compared to the global community—
the memory is marked not by technique, but by the sensation of being surrounded by living magic, in an environment that combines the power of the ocean with a natural spectacle that seems straight out of science fiction.

Some describe the experience as surfing among stars, as the flickering light resembles the night sky reflected on the sea.

For now, there are no official tournaments or widespread practices of bioluminescent night surfing for obvious safety reasons.

However, the idea of surfing glowing waves remains an almost mystical goal for many traveling surfers and ocean artists.

More than a technical achievement, it is an encounter with the sublime, a way of connecting with nature in its most intimate and radiant form.

29

The longest wave in the open ocean, recognized for its consistency and uninterrupted length, is located in Chicama, a small coastal town in northern Peru, in the department of La Libertad, about 600 km north of Lima.

This wave is considered a natural jewel of world surfing, not only because of its length, which can reach up to 2.2 kilometers, but also for the perfection of its break, its regularity during the southern swell season, and the possibility it offers to connect multiple sections in a single ride.

Surfing Chicama is an almost hypnotic experience, where the surfer enters a kind of trance of flow, balance, and endurance that can last several minutes if they manage to maintain the right line and speed.

Chicama's wave is a left-hander (breaking to the left from the surfer's perspective) formed thanks to an exceptional geographical combination: a spiral-shaped rocky point, a sandbank perfectly aligned with the angle of the southern swell, and a curving coastline that allows the wave to "wrap" and maintain its shape over a distance unmatched in open ocean conditions.

While there are other long waves in the world, such as Skeleton Bay in Namibia (which can sometimes be longer but is rare and remote) or Pavones in Costa Rica, Chicama is the most accessible, consistent, and functional of all, with the ability to offer rides lasting over 3 minutes without interruption under optimal conditions.

The full length of the wave is divided into four main sections: Malpaso, Keys, El Point, and El Hombre.

Although they are usually surfed in individual sections,

on days of perfect swell, with good wind alignment and favorable tides, it is possible to connect all four sections in a single continuous ride, covering more than 2 km on the same wave.

Many surfers who have managed to do it describe the sensation as exhausting but deeply rewarding, as the physical demand is high: paddling, performing maneuvers, maintaining speed, reading sections, and continuing for such a long time requires extraordinary endurance.

Chicama is a gentle wave, not particularly tubular or violent, making it ideal for carving maneuvers, wide turns, and technical training.

It is perfect for intermediate to advanced surfers, although it is also very friendly for longboarders and for those looking to improve their ability to read long waves.

It is not a wave of adrenaline due to its size or danger, but rather one of precision, patience, and flow.

The consistency of the swell in the region, between the months of April and October, means that there are entire weeks with waves over a kilometer long available every day.

Historically, Chicama was discovered by the international surfing community in the 1960s, when American and Peruvian surfers began exploring the South Pacific coasts in search of long waves.

Since then, it has become a cult spot within long-wave surfing and a must-visit destination for travelers seeking a different kind of session.

Its fame has grown over the years thanks to documentaries, blogs, social media, and testimonials describing the experience of "endless surfing."

In 2013, the Peruvian government declared the Chicama wave a Protected Natural Heritage site, making it the first wave in the world to be legally protected for its environmental and sporting value.

This means that no infrastructure can be built that would alter its natural formation, and dredging or coastal construction projects that could damage the sandbank are not permitted.

This measure was applauded by the global surfing community as an example of how a natural resource can be conserved from a sporting, ecological, and cultural perspective.

In addition to its surfing value, Chicama has a welcoming and peaceful local atmosphere.

The town, also called Puerto Malabrigo, is small and traditional, with a fishing community and hotels or surf camps that have flourished over the past decades.

It is not a mass tourism destination, which helps maintain it as a place of connection with nature, far from the hustle and bustle of more commercial surf spots.

Chicama has been surfed by some of the best in the world, including legends like Tom Curren, Rob Machado, and more recently, surfers from the professional circuit and renowned freesurfers, although its technical nature and lack of deep barrels keep it off the WSL circuit.

However, that is part of its charm: it is a place to surf for love, not for points.

Surfers from all over the world come here to train, to reconnect with the flow, or simply to fulfill the dream of surfing the longest wave in the world.

30

Surf Enthusiasts.

1. United States
- Surf enthusiasts: 3,000,000
- Famous surfers: Kelly Slater, John John Florence, Carissa Moore, Tom Curren
- Best spots: Malibu, Huntington Beach, Trestles, Santa Cruz, Mavericks (California)

2. Brazil
- Surf enthusiasts: 3,000,000
- Famous surfers: Gabriel Medina, Italo Ferreira, Filipe Toledo, Tatiana Weston-Webb
- Best spots: Maresias, Saquarema, Fernando de Noronha, Praia do Rosa, Itacaré

3. Australia
- Surf enthusiasts: 1,700,000
- Famous surfers: Mick Fanning, Stephanie Gilmore, Joel Parkinson, Tyler Wright
- Best spots: Gold Coast (Snapper Rocks), Bells Beach, Byron Bay, Margaret River

4. United Kingdom
- Surf enthusiasts: 500,000
- Famous surfers: Reubyn Ash, Alan Stokes, Lucy Campbell
- Best spots: Fistral Beach (Newquay), Perranporth, Polzeath, Thurso (Scotland)

5. France
- Surf enthusiasts: 450,000
- Famous surfers: Jérémy Florès, Johanne Defay, Michel Bourez
- Best spots: Hossegor, Biarritz, Lacanau, La Gravière, Belharra

6. South Africa
- Surf enthusiasts: 420,000
- Famous surfers: Jordy Smith, Shaun Tomson, Bianca Buitendag
- Best spots: Jeffreys Bay, Dungeons, Durban, Muizenberg

7. Spain
- Surf enthusiasts: 300,000
- Famous surfers: Aritz Aranburu, Lucía Martiño, Leticia Canales
- Best spots: Mundaka, Zarautz, El Palmar, Playa de Somo, Las Américas (Tenerife)

8. Portugal
- Surf enthusiasts: 200,000
- Famous surfers: Frederico Morais, Teresa Bonvalot, Nic von Rupp
- Best spots: Nazaré, Peniche (Supertubos), Ericeira, Carcavelos

9. New Zealand
- Surf enthusiasts: 145,000
- Famous surfers: Ella Williams, Ricardo Christie, Paige Hareb
- Best spots: Raglan (Manu Bay), Piha, Gisborne, Mount Maunganui

10. Japan
- Surf enthusiasts: 120,000
- Famous surfers: Kanoa Igarashi, Hiroto Ohhara, Mahina Maeda
- Best spots: Chiba, Shonan, Miyazaki, Niijima, Okinawa

11. Peru
- Surf enthusiasts: 110,000
- Famous surfers: Sofía Mulánovich, Lucca Mesinas, Miguel Tudela
- Best spots: Chicama, Punta Hermosa, Máncora, Punta Rocas, Lobitos

12. Costa Rica
- Surf enthusiasts: 95,000
- Famous surfers: Carlos Muñoz, Leilani McGonagle, Brisa Hennessy
- Best spots: Santa Teresa, Playa Hermosa, Pavones, Tamarindo, Dominical

13. Indonesia
- Surf enthusiasts: 85,000
- Famous surfers: Rizal Tanjung, Oney Anwar, Mega Semadhi
- Best spots: Uluwatu, Padang Padang, G-Land, Mentawai, Nias

14. Mexico
- Surf enthusiasts: 80,000
- Famous surfers: Jhony Corzo, Alan Cleland Jr., Shelby Detmers
- Best spots: Puerto Escondido, Sayulita, La Ticla, Barra de la Cruz

15. Italy
- Surf enthusiasts: 45,000
- Famous surfers: Leonardo Fioravanti, Roberto D'Amico, Francesca Rubegni
- Best spots: Sardinia (Capo Mannu), Levanto, Tuscany (Versilia), Lazio (Santa Marinella)

16. Netherlands
- Surf enthusiasts: 40,000
- Famous surfers: Yannick de Jager, Kaspar Hamminga
- Best spots: Scheveningen, Zandvoort, Wijk aan Zee, Domburg

17. Canada
- Surf enthusiasts: 35,000
- Famous surfers: Pete Devries, Noah Cohen, Catherine Bruhwiler
- Best spots: Tofino (British Columbia), Lawrencetown Beach

(Nova Scotia), Long Beach (Ucluelet)

18. Germany
- Surf enthusiasts: ~30,000
- Famous surfers: Marlon Lipke (German-Portuguese), Janina Zeitler (river surfing), Gerry Schlegel
- Best spots: Eisbach (Munich, river surfing), Sylt (North Sea), St. Peter-Ording

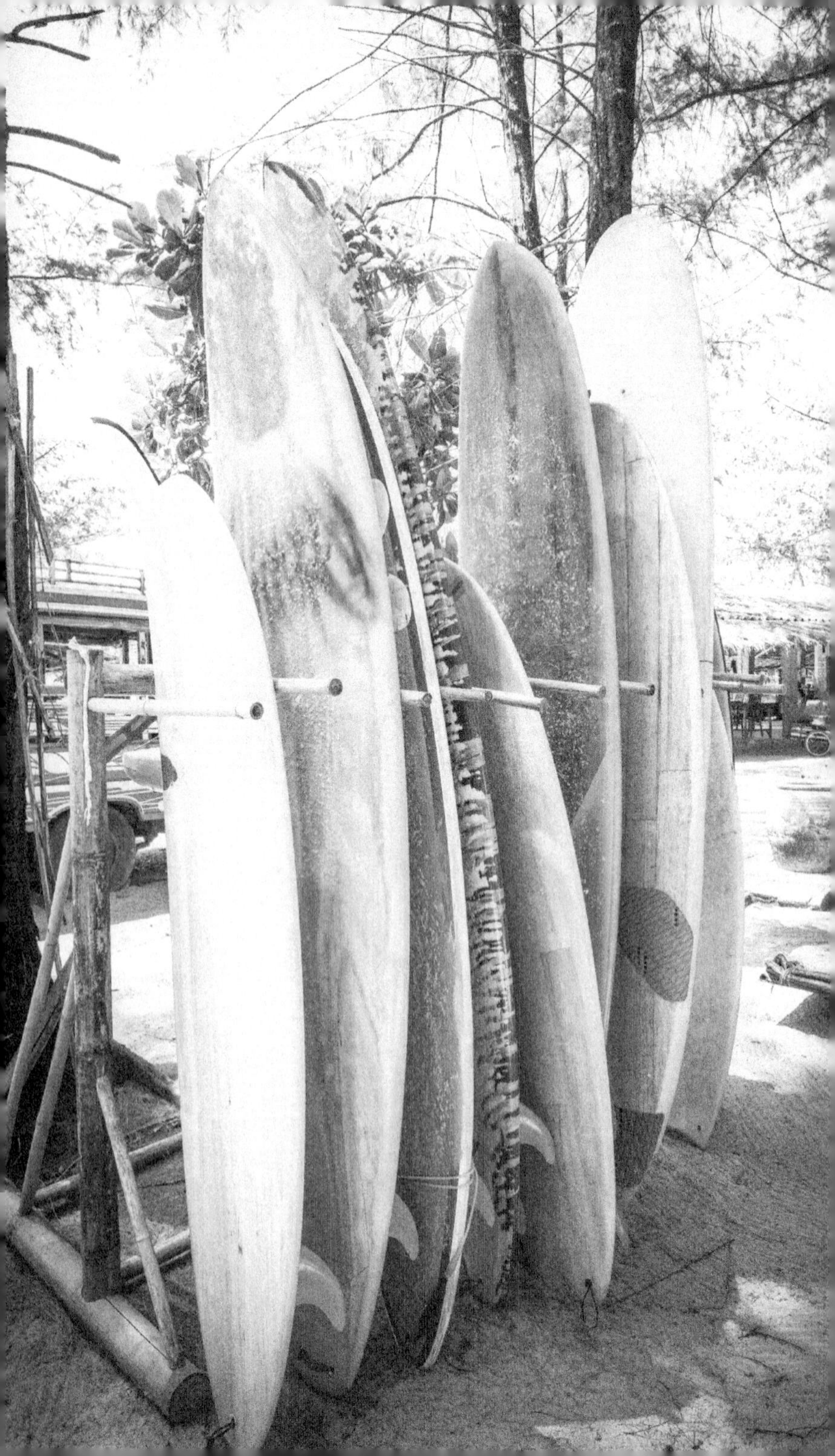

31

Surfing in the Arctic surrounded by icebergs is one of the most extreme, inhospitable, and visually stunning manifestations of modern surfing.

It is not a common or mass phenomenon but rather a frontier discipline practiced by surfers who are not merely seeking big or perfect waves, but experiences that challenge the limits of the human body, tolerance to cold, logistics, and the ability to connect with landscapes that seem to come from another planet.

In this environment, where the sea is at near-freezing temperatures, the wind slices the skin like blades, and ice blocks float like moving mountains, every paddle stroke is a statement of respect for nature in its wildest form.

Surfing in the Arctic involves not only the cold but also unpredictable conditions, unique natural dangers, and very specific mental and technical preparation.

The waves can form in remote fjords, in the northern bays of Norway, Greenland, Iceland, or even in areas near the Arctic Circle in Canada and Russia.

These waves, when they appear, do so suddenly, often without accurate forecasting, with icy winds and a dark, dense sea.

Surfers who dare to enter the water under these conditions usually wear 6 mm wetsuits with hoods, thick booties and gloves, internal heating layers, and petroleum jelly on sensitive areas such as the face to protect themselves from hypothermia.

One of the pioneers of this type of surfing was American

adventure photographer Chris Burkard, who has documented surfers in places like the Lofoten Islands (Norway), the Svalbard Archipelago, and unexplored areas of Iceland and Alaska.

Although Burkard is not a professional surfer, he has traveled with surfing legends like Ramón Navarro, Patrick Millin, Timmy Reyes, Emil Hansen, and Dane Gudauskas, who have surfed waves under falling snow, with northern lights illuminating the sky and surrounded by icebergs cracking and breaking under the pressure of the swell.

On some occasions, surfers have had to walk for hours through snowy landscapes carrying their boards, cut through ice blocks to access the water, or even surf among floating chunks that can break a board with a single collision.

One of the most extreme spots documented is in Tasiilaq, Greenland, where waves form in narrow bays bordered by glaciers and snow-covered mountains.

Surfing has also taken place in Unstad, in the Lofoten Islands, Norway, where despite the freezing latitude, consistent waves are generated thanks to the area's exposure to the Norwegian Sea.

In Iceland, beaches like Thorli and certain secret spots in the south have been the setting for sessions with water temperatures between 1°C and 4°C, where surfers' breath vapor mixes with frozen dew on their hair.

Arctic surfing is not about competitive performance, but about full immersion in an overwhelming environment.

It is an introspective, almost spiritual experience, where silence reigns, waves seem to emerge from the abyss, and the sense of solitude is complete.

There is no crowd, no infrastructure, and often not even

phone coverage, as this is surfing based on exploration, discovery, and endurance.

Several professional surfers have taken part in Arctic expeditions as part of documentaries or photographic projects.

Mick Fanning, Australian three-time world champion, surfed in Iceland for a Red Bull production, facing freezing waves in the middle of a snowstorm.

Torren Martyn, known for his fluid style on twin-fin boards, has also made trips through cold regions where the priority was the search for virgin waves, not comfort.

Mark Mathews, a big wave specialist, has stated that some of the toughest sessions of his life were in icy seas where every wipeout was a battle against thermal shock.

Moreover, Arctic surfing has been incorporated into climate activism narratives.

Surfers like Ramón Navarro and Iceland's Heiða Rún Sigurðardóttir have used their expeditions to draw attention to glacier melt, plastic pollution in remote areas, and the urgent need to protect fragile seas that until recently were nearly inaccessible.

In this sense, surfing among icebergs is not only a physical and aesthetic feat but also an act of bearing witness to global change.

Visually, these sessions are unique: images of a surfer gliding over a black wave, with snow-covered mountains in the background and a translucent blue iceberg just a few meters away, hold an unmatched evocative power.

32

Jackson Dorian, born on September 22, 2006, in Hawaii, is one of the brightest young prospects in contemporary surfing and, at the same time, a media and sports phenomenon shaped by his lineage.

He is the son of legendary big wave surfer Shane Dorian, an iconic figure in big wave surfing and a pioneer in modern high-performance training for surfers, and the godson of eleven-time world champion Kelly Slater.

Growing up in an environment where surfing is more than just a sport—it's a lifestyle and a cultural heritage—made Jackson practically destined to stand out.

He began sliding on a surfboard at the age of three, and by five, he was already being filmed surfing small waves with an unusual skill for his age.

His natural talent, combined with his father's technical guidance and access to some of the best waves on the planet, allowed him to progress rapidly.

By the age of 10, Jackson Dorian was already participating in official tournaments like the Keiki Classic, an event created and organized by his own father to promote youth surfing in Hawaii.

He didn't just participate: he won his division, and his style caught attention for its blend of technical control, fluidity, and creativity.

Far from limiting himself to the local junior circuit, Jackson began traveling from a very young age: he has surfed in places like Australia, the Maldives, Fiji, Mexico, Japan, and California, gaining experience in different types of waves and conditions, from soft beach breaks to sharp reef breaks.

He has also practiced other sports that complement his technique on the board, such as skateboarding (which develops balance and turns) and snowboarding (which gives him control on slippery surfaces).

One of his most extraordinary feats came in 2021, when at just 13 years old he managed to surf at Jaws (Pe'ahi) on the island of Maui, considered one of the most dangerous waves in the world.

It is a world-class wave usually reserved for experienced adults, requiring extreme paddling technique, precise ocean reading, and unshakable mental fortitude.

The mere fact that a 13-year-old would drop into Jaws not only surprised the surfing world but elevated his status to that of a young legend in the making.

Jackson was captured on camera confidently riding waves several meters high, with a command of the lineup and a level of maturity far beyond his years.

That session was considered historic and was widely covered by outlets such as Surfer Magazine and Stab.

In terms of professional projection, Jackson has been sponsored from a young age by major brands like Billabong, Slater Designs, and Reef, which reflects not only his quality as an athlete but also his media impact.

He maintains a strong presence on social media, where he documents his sessions, travels, and training, connecting with a community of young surfers around the world.

His YouTube channel and Instagram account have served to showcase his evolution, from early days in wave pools like Waco and The Surf Ranch to his experiences in remote seas with challenging waves.

Despite the weight of being "Shane Dorian's son," Jackson has proven himself to be a surfer with his own identity, without relying on his last name to make his way.

As for other curiosities, Jackson stands out not only for his skills but also for his humility, work ethic, and charismatic personality.

He enjoys spending time with his family, has a passion for music, and is an advocate for marine conservation, having participated in beach cleanups and conservation projects.

His youth means he has not yet earned professional titles in the Championship Tour (CT), but he is widely regarded as a future star of the World Surf League (WSL).

33

There are extreme cases that show that neither height nor body build determines talent or success.

Among these examples, two opposites stand out:
Derek Hooley, as the tallest recorded professional surfer, and Tatiana Weston-Webb and Adriano de Souza, as the shortest, who have made history in high-level surfing despite their physical differences.

Derek Hooley, standing at an imposing 2.03 meters (6'8"), represents a unique case in contemporary surfing.

His size, far above the average in the sport, has made him an easily recognizable figure in lineups, especially in the realm of big wave surfing, where his weight and strength offer an advantage in paddling, stability, and drive.

Although his participation in the official World Surf League (WSL) circuit has been limited, Derek has gained notoriety in freesurf sessions and alternative events where powerful wave surfing is the main focus.

His surfing style is more linear and solid than acrobatic, which is logical given his build.

Aerial maneuvers or quick transitions on small waves can be more challenging for someone of his height, but his performance in big waves such as Puerto Escondido, Mavericks, or Outer Reef Oahu has been admirable.

His story also serves to highlight that surfing does not have a fixed physical mold and that body diversity enriches the sport just as much as the diversity of styles.

At the other end of the spectrum is Tatiana Weston-Webb,

a surfer born in Hawaii who represents Brazil on the WSL women's circuit.

Standing at 1.57 meters (5'2"), Tatiana is likely the shortest professional surfer on the current tour.

Her height, far from being a disadvantage, has been an asset in many technical aspects.

Her lower center of gravity allows her to maintain greater control in critical sections of the wave and to execute quick, compact, high-performance maneuvers with great precision.

Tatiana has been at the top of women's world surfing from a very young age and is known for her explosive energy, determination, and charisma.

She has achieved multiple podium finishes on the Championship Tour and represented Brazil at the Tokyo 2020 Olympic Games.

Her small stature has not affected her international projection, and she has been featured in global advertising campaigns for brands like Rip Curl, Red Bull, and Oakley, as well as being an active voice for female empowerment within the sport.

On the men's circuit, the shortest professional surfer to reach the top is undoubtedly Adriano de Souza, nicknamed "Mineirinho," who, at 1.67 meters (5'6"), became WSL world champion in 2015, defeating much taller and flashier competitors.

Adriano is a symbol of discipline, humility, and strategy.

Raised in a humble neighborhood of Guarujá, Brazil, he began surfing on a used board given to him by his older brother.

His perseverance, mental strength, and tactical approach led him to become one of the leading figures of the famous "Brazilian Storm," the generation of Brazilian surfers who revolutionized the sport over the past decade.

His shorter stature gave him an advantage in executing tight maneuvers in critical sections of the wave, and his physical power compensated for any apparent disadvantage against taller rivals.

Adriano's victory at the Pipe Masters and his crowning as world champion not only earned him global recognition but also opened the doors for thousands of young surfers from underprivileged backgrounds to dream of reaching the elite level without needing a perfect body or early sponsorships.

34

**In 2022, surfing reached a new milestone
by moving into the microgravity environment.**

For the first time, a professional surfer experienced the sensation of gliding on a board in a weightless environment, thanks to a parabolic flight that simulated zero gravity.

This achievement was made possible through a collaboration between a professional surfer, aerospace engineers, and the company Novespace, which operates the Airbus A310 Zero G.

The parabolic flight recreates the state of weightlessness during an airplane flight by alternating very steep climbs and free-fall descents.

During these maneuvers, weightlessness is recreated onboard the plane for approximately 22 seconds.

In zero-gravity flights used for scientific research, this maneuver is repeated multiple times and can also simulate lunar and Martian gravity during certain parabolas.

For this experience, a specially adapted surfboard was designed, lighter and equipped with special grips, allowing the surfer to maintain balance and perform maneuvers in the air.

During the flight, the surfer used the intervals of weightlessness to simulate surfing movements and postures, defying the laws of terrestrial physics.

This initiative not only represented a technical and sporting achievement but also opened new possibilities for training surfers under extreme conditions and for researching body movements in microgravity.

35

The Most Prestigious Surf Tournaments.

1. Vans Triple Crown of Surfing (Hawaii, USA)
This event consists of three competitions on Oahu's North Shore: the Hawaiian Pro in Haleiwa, the World Cup of Surfing at Sunset Beach, and the Pipeline Masters at Banzai Pipeline. It is considered one of the most demanding tests in professional surfing. The total prize pool exceeds $740,000, including additional bonuses for overall champions.

2. Billabong Pro Teahupo'o (Tahiti, French Polynesia)
Held at the feared Teahupo'o wave, known for its danger and perfect barrels. Prize money has reached up to $607,800, attracting surfers like Kelly Slater, Gabriel Medina, and Mick Fanning.

3. J-Bay Open (Jeffreys Bay, South Africa)
Famous for its long right-handers, this event has been won by legends such as Kelly Slater and Mick Fanning. Prizes have varied, reaching up to $425,000 in some editions.

4. Hurley Pro at Trestles (California, USA)
Held at the waves of Trestles, it is known for its consistency and quality. The total prize has been $579,000, with valuable points for the world ranking.

5. Corona Open J-Bay (Jeffreys Bay, South Africa)
Another competition at Jeffreys Bay, notable for its history and competitive level. Surfers like Filipe Toledo and Lakey Peterson have shined at this event.

6. O'Neill World Cup of Surfing (Sunset Beach, Hawaii)
Part of the Triple Crown, this event at Sunset Beach is known for its big waves and has been won by surfers like Makuakai Rothman and Raoni Monteiro.

The prizes have varied, with additional bonuses for the top performers in the series.

7. Margaret River Pro (Australia)
Held in Western Australia, it is known for its powerful waves and challenging conditions. It is a key stop on the world tour.

8. Rip Curl Pro Bells Beach (Australia)
The oldest event in professional surfing, held in Victoria, Australia. Winners include Mick Fanning and Stephanie Gilmore.

9. Surf Ranch Pro (California, USA)
Held at the artificial wave pool created by Kelly Slater, it offers controlled conditions and has been part of the world tour.

10. Saquarema Pro (Brazil)
Located in Rio de Janeiro, it is known for its vibrant atmosphere and consistent waves. Brazilian surfers like Gabriel Medina have excelled here.

11. Tahiti Pro (Teahupo'o, French Polynesia)
Another competition at Teahupo'o, famous for its deep and challenging barrels. It is a true test for the best surfers in the world.

12. Quiksilver Pro France (Hossegor, France)
Located on the French Atlantic coast, it is famous for its beach breaks and has been part of the world tour.

13. Spring Surfest Las Américas Pro (Tenerife, Spain)
This event combines sport, culture, and social activism. It includes competitions such as the Eurocup and the Euromaster, with prizes reaching €25,000.

15. La Vaca Gigante (Santander, Spain)
A big wave competition held when conditions reach between 6 and 8 meters. Twenty-four international surfers compete for a prize of €12,000.

16. US Open of Surfing (Huntington Beach, California, USA)

This tournament is held in Huntington Beach, known as "Surf City USA," in California, and is one of the oldest and most popular events in professional surfing. It is part of the WSL Qualifying Series (QS) and attracts thousands of spectators with its urban atmosphere, concerts, and cultural activities. The prize money varies depending on the category but usually ranges between $100,000 and $300,000, divided between male and female competitors. Notable surfers such as Kanoa Igarashi, Caroline Marks, Sage Erickson, Yago Dora, and Tatiana Weston-Webb have participated. The wave is a consistent and versatile beach break that allows for all kinds of maneuvers, although the real challenge lies in standing out among dozens of competitors in often unpredictable conditions.

17. Haleiwa Challenger (Hawaii, USA)

Located on the North Shore of Oahu, at the iconic Haleiwa beach, this tournament is part of the WSL Challenger Series, the circuit that determines who qualifies for the Championship Tour. Although not as extreme as Pipeline, Haleiwa offers powerful and fast waves, ideal for showcasing technique and consistency. Prizes have ranged between $100,000 and $200,000, with surfers like Leonardo Fioravanti, Ezekiel Lau, Bettylou Sakura Johnson, and Gabriela Bryan competing in recent editions. It is a highly followed event due to its importance for qualification and because it takes place during the Hawaiian winter season, where the conditions are intense and the level of competition is extremely high.

18. ISA World Surfing Games

This world championship organized by the International Surfing Association changes location every year and has been held in places like Japan, France, and recently in El Salvador. Unlike CT or QS events, this tournament does not award cash prizes but offers an even greater reward: Olympic qualification for surfers from different nations. It is a national team competition where prestige and collective strategy play a key role. Names like Gabriel Medina, Carissa Moore, Italo Ferreira, Jordy Smith, and Stephanie Gilmore have competed here. It is a tournament that highlights the Olympic spirit and the global unity of surfing.

19. Red Bull Magnitude (Hawaii, USA)

This event runs throughout the entire big wave season in Hawaii, at spots like Jaws (Pe'ahi), Waimea Bay, and other outer reefs. Unlike traditional tournaments with set dates, Red Bull Magnitude evaluates the best women's surf sessions over several months through a judging panel that reviews clips and documented performances. The prize pool has been approximately $50,000 to $100,000, with special awards for the best wave, the most radical drop, and the most consistent performance. Athletes such as Justine Dupont, Keala Kennelly, Paige Alms, and Emily Erickson participate, and it is one of the few tournaments dedicated exclusively to women's big wave surfing.

19. Vans Duct Tape Invitational

This alternative and culturally significant tournament travels to different countries, including Mexico, France, Spain, and the United States. It is a classic longboard event that prioritizes style, creativity, and elegance over traditional competition. The prize pool ranges between $20,000 and $60,000, depending on the edition, and brings together the best in longboard surfing in a relaxed, artistic, and collaborative atmosphere. Names like Joel Tudor, Harrison Roach, Honolua Blomfield, and Justin Quintal have participated. In addition to the tournament itself, the event includes activities such as exhibitions, workshops, and beach cleanups, with a strong community and environmental focus.

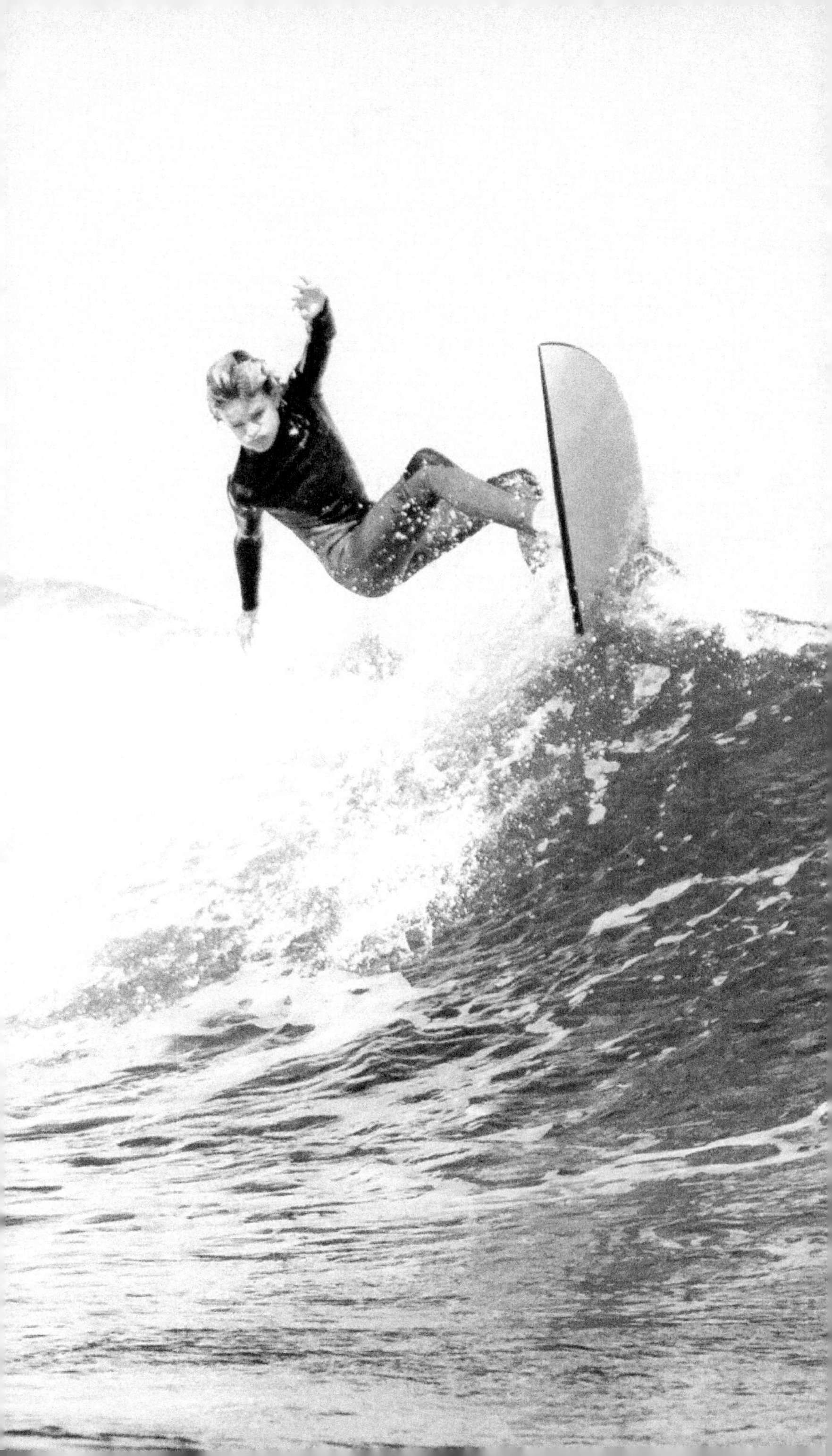

36

Benji Brand.

A South African surfer based in Hawaii, he achieved a feat rarely seen in surfing history by linking more than five consecutive barrels on a single wave at Skeleton Bay, Namibia, one of the most legendary and remote places on the planet for such accomplishments.

Skeleton Bay is known for offering what many consider the longest and most perfect left-hand barrel in the world, a natural phenomenon that happens only a few times a year when swell and wind conditions align precisely.

On one of those epic days, Benji rode inside a wave lasting more than two minutes, getting barreled and spit out multiple times through deep, hollow sections, until he accomplished something that seemed almost unreal: more than five clean barrels in a single ride, without interruption, without losing speed, and without leaving the critical line.

Benji Brand was born in South Africa but grew up among the waves of Hawaii, where he developed a clean, powerful, and technical style, with a particular inclination toward deep barrels.

From an early age, he showed uncommon maturity on the board, specializing in tube reading and decision-making under pressure.

His career has not been focused on the Championship Tour (CT) like many other professional surfers, but rather on a path as a professional freesurfer, occasionally competing in QS (Qualifying Series) events but standing out mainly for his exploration trips, his film projects, and his remarkable ability to find and ride some of the best waves on the planet.

He is known for being reserved, disciplined, and obsessive about technique.

His approach to surfing barrels is surgical: he stays in the deepest part of the cavern without losing stability, exiting precisely at the right moment before being swallowed by the foam.

This skill has made him a favorite among surf filmmakers, appearing in numerous movies, documentaries, and viral videos.

His session at Skeleton Bay became iconic not only for the number of barrels but for the fluidity with which he connected them.

The wave he rode was captured by a drone, and the video went viral within the international surf community: you can see Benji disappearing into the first barrel, shooting out and immediately sliding into a second, then a third, fourth, and fifth, without his speed ever being compromised.

Even after the fifth barrel, he continued surfing for over a minute, leading some to estimate that the wave covered between 1.5 and 2 kilometers in total distance.

That wave was considered by many as the perfect wave, and Benji Brand as the surfer who has come closest to what would be a "marathon inside a single barrel."

Although he did not receive an official title or specific financial reward for that moment, his name was forever etched into surfing history.

Since then, he has been invited to special tournaments and productions alongside some of the world's best surfers and remains a benchmark for pure barrel-riding technique.

Benji is also an advocate for sustainable surfing and has

worked with organizations focused on coastal conservation in Africa and the Pacific.

Despite maintaining a low profile on social media, he is highly respected among his peers, and many CT champions cite him as one of the surfers with the best "line reading" (reading the barrel line) on the planet.

In a sport where spectacle is often associated with aerials or powerful turns, Benji has proven that the art of surfing barrels with elegance remains one of the purest and most challenging expressions of surfing.

37

Andrew Cotton.

A British surfer born in Devon in 1979, he is known as one of the bravest and most respected names in the world of big wave surfing, with a career marked by extreme feats, unwavering dedication, and also one of the most harrowing accidents in recent surfing history.

In November 2017, Cotton was violently thrown by a wave over 20 meters high at Nazaré, Portugal—the mecca of giant waves—during a session that seemed epic but ended in a near-death experience.

The wipeout was so brutal that the footage went viral within hours, with outlets like the BBC, The Guardian, and Surfer Magazine broadcasting the exact moment Andrew was launched by the lip of the wave like a rag doll, disappeared into the foam, and finally reemerged motionless as his safety team rushed in to rescue him.

The wave was massive, probably in the 75-foot (23-meter) range, and broke with vertical violence, causing his board to detach and his body to plummet from the top as if falling from a seven-story building.

The impact was so severe that he fractured his back, suffering a vertebral compression injury.

Even so, thanks to the quick response of the rescue team—especially the jet ski operator—he was brought to shore and taken to the hospital, where he remained immobilized but conscious and out of life-threatening danger.

From his hospital bed, he posted a message on social media thanking everyone for their support and expressing gratitude for being alive, demonstrating the positive spirit that has always defined him.

Andrew Cotton's story does not begin at Nazaré, but in the cold waters of the United Kingdom, where he learned to surf along the North Devon coast, at beaches like Croyde and Saunton Sands.

He worked as a plumber for years while training in his free time, and little by little, he specialized in big waves, becoming one of the few British surfers recognized worldwide in this field.

His rise began when he started collaborating with the legendary Garrett McNamara, who brought him onto his giant wave hunting team at Nazaré.

Cotton often drove the jet ski for Garrett, but soon he began to take on the waves himself, eventually earning his own place among the elite of big wave surfing.

Cotton has surfed at all of the planet's extreme destinations: Mullaghmore in Ireland, Jaws in Hawaii, Cortes Bank in California, and of course Praia do Norte in Nazaré, which became his second home.

His style is technical, controlled, and precise, perfectly suited for long, heavy lines where reading the wave can mean the difference between success and a trip to the hospital.

After his accident in 2017, many thought he would retire, but in 2018 he returned to the water, stronger and more determined than ever.

His recovery was a model of discipline: physiotherapy, functional training, a focused mindset, and a deep love for what he does.

Cotton stated that he didn't want his story to end with a

wipeout, but with a new wave that would define him better than any accident.

In addition to being a surfer, he is an environmental ambassador, motivational speaker, and lecturer.

He has spoken at schools, sporting events, and companies about the value of fear, resilience, and passion.

He has also worked with the WSL on big wave safety projects and has appeared in documentaries for the BBC and Red Bull TV.

On a personal level, he is a family man, living between England and Portugal, and maintains a simple life focused on the ocean and inspiring others.

38

Maya Gabeira, a Brazilian surfer born in Rio de Janeiro in 1987, made history in world surfing in 2018 by becoming the first woman to surf a wave over 20 meters (66 feet), specifically at Nazaré, Portugal, one of the most feared waves on the planet.

That same year, she was certified by the Guinness World Records as the woman who had surfed the largest wave in the world, an achievement that broke not only physical and technical barriers but also symbolic ones in a sport historically dominated by men.

The wave Maya surfed was generated during one of the largest swells ever recorded at Praia do Norte in Nazaré, a place where the seafloor—a combination of a submarine canyon and a sandbank—creates waves of enormous size and power.

Her drop was clean, technical, and challenging, and although many did not realize it at the time, that moment was the culmination of a brutal story of perseverance.

Maya Gabeira did not arrive at that wave as an overnight star, but as a woman marked by a near-fatal experience in 2013, also at Nazaré, where she was knocked down by a giant wave, lost consciousness underwater, and was rescued from the brink of death by her partner Carlos Burle.

That wipeout caused her a severe leg injury and multiple physical and emotional aftereffects, keeping her out of the water for a long period.

Her comeback was not just physical, but also mental: She retrained her body, strengthened her muscles, overcame deep traumas, and returned to train at the very place where she had nearly died.

The 2018 record was more than a sporting victory: it was redemption, a response to fear, and a proclamation of courage.

Maya herself has said that that wave was her way of reclaiming control over what she loved, and she did it with the strength of someone who is not content just to survive, but who seeks to be reborn even stronger.

Meanwhile, Layne Beachley, an Australian surfer born in 1972, is one of the most dominant figures in the history of women's surfing, with seven world titles, six of them consecutive.

But one of her lesser-known and most astonishing records happened during an epic session in Australia, where she surfed over 300 waves in a single day, setting the record for the most waves surfed by a woman in one session.

This achievement, although less publicized than surfing a giant wave, demands monumental physical and mental endurance.

It requires strength, stamina, focus, controlled heart rate, positioning strategy, and an almost superhuman energy.

Spending hours upon hours paddling, turning, standing up on the board, falling, and trying again is a feat of consistency that goes beyond spectacle; it is a tribute to endurance, an intimate connection with the ocean, and pure love for surfing.

Layne is not only a competitive champion but also a powerful voice for gender equality, mental wellness, and female empowerment.

After retiring from the professional circuit, she founded the "Awaken" Academy, focused on personal growth and leadership, and has served as a surfing ambassador in mental health and wellness campaigns.

Her record of 300 waves in a single day was not a publicity stunt or an Olympic mark; it was a reflection of her tenacious personality, her uncompromising discipline, and her way of inspiring without words.

She did it because she could, because she wanted to, and because she knew that no wave is ridden alone: each one is part of a dance with the ocean, where what matters is not fame, but endurance.

39

In the history of professional surfing, few moments have reached such a high level of technical and symbolic perfection as when Kelly Slater achieved a perfect score of 20/20 in the final of the 2003 Pipe Masters, one of the most prestigious tournaments in the world, held at Banzai Pipeline on the North Shore of Oahu, Hawaii.

This event is famous for its powerful, hollow waves that break over a sharp reef, and only the most technical and courageous surfers stand out there.

In that historic final, Slater—already a multiple-time world champion—showed why he is considered the greatest surfer of all time.

In spectacular conditions, with deep barrels requiring perfect wave reading and absolute control, Kelly scored two waves with 10.0 from all the judges, something extremely rare in competition.

His first 10 came from a critical takeoff and a clean barrel with a perfect exit.

But it was his second wave that left everyone speechless: a risky line, with multiple sections, where he completely disappeared inside the barrel and emerged just before it closed out.

In total, Slater scored 20 points out of 20 possible, entering history as one of the few surfers to achieve that ideal score, and the first to do so in a CT final under maximum pressure.

This achievement was not an isolated one.

Kelly Slater is known for his ability to elevate his performance at critical moments and has won the Pipe Masters multiple times.

His mastery at Pipeline is based on a combination of innate talent, an obsession with technical improvement, and a deep understanding of the wave.

Pipeline does not forgive mistakes, and that 2003 final not only crowned Slater once again as the king of that break, but also marked one of the most iconic performances in the history of the World Surf League.

On the other hand, a completely different but equally significant achievement for its cultural and innovative impact was accomplished by Zoltan "The Magician" Torkos, a Californian surfer who landed the first documented kickflip on a surfboard, a maneuver imported from skateboarding that until then was considered almost impossible to perform on a wave.

The kickflip is a trick where the board flips along its longitudinal axis while the surfer jumps, requiring almost surgical synchronization between the feet, body, and the speed of the wave.

Although some surfing purists questioned the validity or relevance of the trick, the alternative community and many freesurfers celebrated it as a milestone.

Zoltan landed the kickflip in 2011 after years of attempts and with the incentive of a challenge launched by TransWorld SURF magazine, which offered $10,000 to whoever could successfully complete it with video evidence.

His board was slightly adapted to facilitate the rotation, with a design that maintained buoyancy while allowing a quicker takeoff.

The video of his maneuver went viral within the surfing

community, generating both admiration and controversy, but undoubtedly placing him in history as an innovator, a figure who expanded the boundaries of what can be done on a wave.

Zoltan Torkos is not a WSL competitor or a barrel champion, but a creative, passionate surfer with a hybrid vision between skateboarding and surfing.

He has performed multiple unconventional aerial maneuvers, given talks on motivation and creativity, and remained active in the scene as a kind of alternative surf artist.

His nickname "The Magician" comes not only from his tricks but also from his playful personality and his drive to amaze.

In interviews, he has said that he doesn't just want to surf waves: he wants people to say "Wow!" when they see him.

40

Surf made its Olympic debut at the Tokyo 2020 Games, held in 2021 due to the pandemic.

The competitions took place from July 25 to 28 at Tsurigasaki Beach, Ichinomiya, Chiba Prefecture, Japan.

Twenty men and twenty women from eighteen countries participated, competing in the shortboard discipline.

In the men's category, Brazilian Ítalo Ferreira won the gold medal, defeating Japan's Kanoa Igarashi, who took silver.

Australian Owen Wright claimed the bronze.

In the women's category, American Carissa Moore was crowned Olympic champion, beating South African Bianca Buitendag, who took silver.

Japanese surfer Amuro Tsuzuki secured the bronze.

The competition format included initial non-elimination rounds, followed by direct elimination rounds from the round of 16 through to the final.

Each heat lasted between 20 and 35 minutes, and the two best waves of each surfer were scored from 0 to 10 by a panel of judges.

Scores were based on the difficulty, innovation, variety, speed, power, and flow of the maneuvers.

Surfing's debut at the Olympic Games was a historic milestone, highlighting the inclusion of the sport.

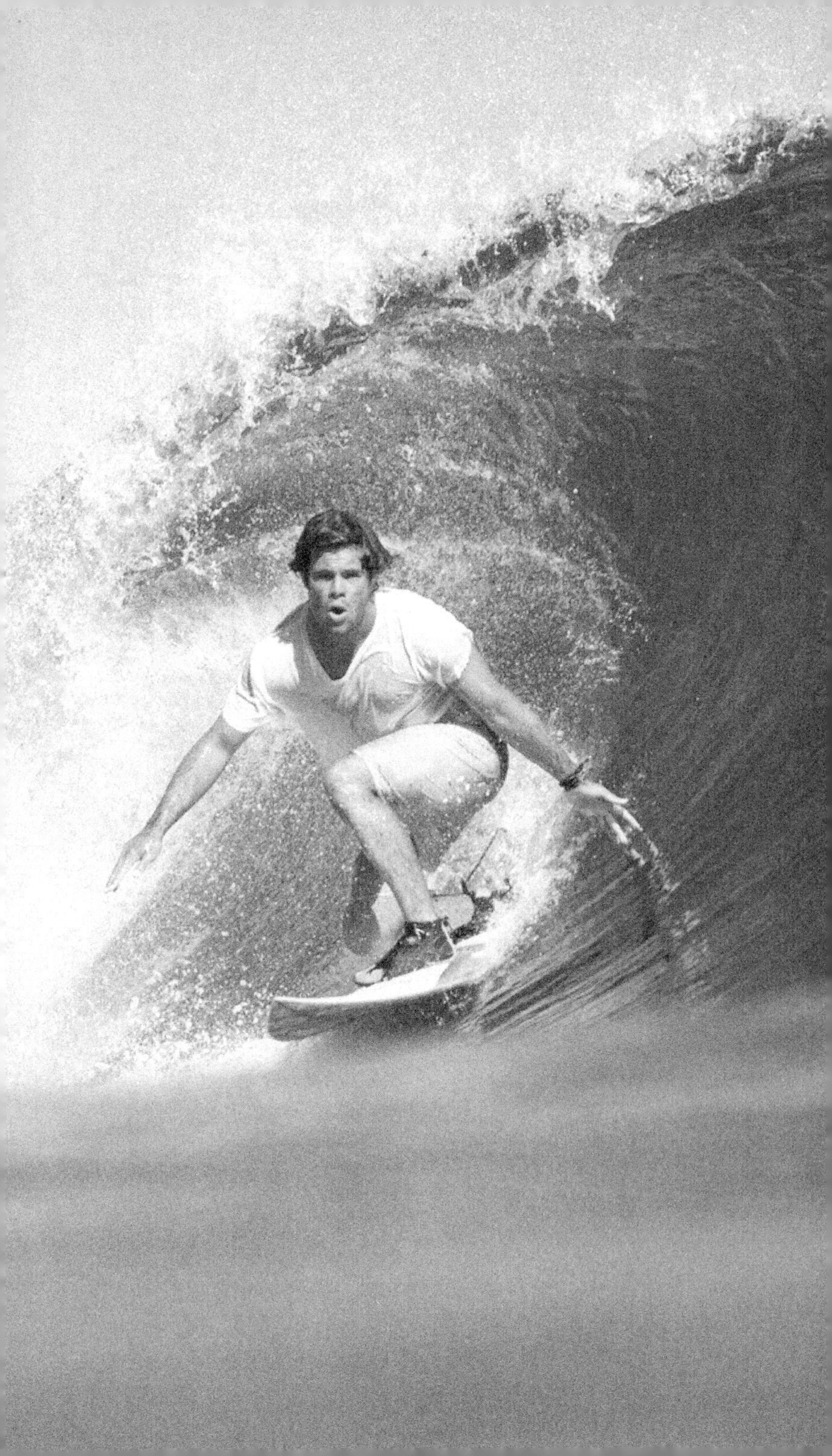

41

"Urban surfing" is an emerging practice that involves surfing in urban environments, such as canals, rivers, and public fountains, especially after torrential rains that create currents suitable for wave formation.

This style has gained popularity in various cities around the world, adapting traditional surfing to urban contexts and taking advantage of existing infrastructure or natural phenomena to practice the sport.

A notable example is the Eisbach in Munich, Germany, a 2-kilometer-long artificial canal that runs through the Englischer Garten.

Since the 1970s, surfers have taken advantage of a stationary wave formed by the canal's current to practice surfing.

Although initially prohibited, surfing at the Eisbach was officially authorized in 2010, making it a key reference point for urban surfing in Europe.

In Rotterdam, the Netherlands, the RiF010 project was developed, an artificial wave pool installed in the Steigersgracht canal.

This project, inaugurated in 2015, allows residents to practice surfing in the heart of the city, integrating the sport into the urban environment and promoting recreational water activities.

In Zurich, Switzerland, surfers have implemented a pulley system known as "upstream surfing" in the Limmat River, allowing them to surf against the current using a fixed rope and the force of the water.

This innovation has adapted surfing to river conditions, offering a unique experience in an urban environment.

In Austria, the city of Graz has two artificial waves on the Mur River, built in 2001 and reconstructed in 2004, which have been regularly used for surfing.

Similarly, in Salzburg, there is the "Almwelle," a customized wave on the Alm Canal, specifically designed for urban surfing.

In Norway, several cities have developed river waves for surfing, such as the "Bulken Wave" in Voss, the "Sluppen Wave" in Trondheim, and the "Sarp Wave" in Sarpsborg.

These projects have adapted surfing to the country's river environments, taking advantage of natural conditions and promoting the sport in non-coastal areas.

42

Cloudbreak, located off the island of Tavarua in Fiji, is globally recognized for offering some of the most challenging and spectacular waves in surfing.

This left-hand reef break is famous for its long, powerful barrels, which at times allow surfers to experience multiple barrel sections on a single wave, known as "double barrels."

During the historic swell of May 2018, Cloudbreak delivered exceptional conditions that allowed several professional surfers to enjoy prolonged and consecutive barrels.

In sessions documented by specialized media, waves were observed offering barrel sections lasting more than 10 seconds each, allowing surfers to link two barrels on a single wave.

Among those who stood out in these sessions were surfers like Soli Bailey, Timo, and Caity, who made the most of the epic conditions during that period.

Additionally, in June 2015, during the Fiji Pro of the World Surf League, Australian surfer Owen Wright made history by achieving two perfect 20/20 scores in a single competition at Cloudbreak.

His performance included multiple deep and prolonged barrels, demonstrating this wave's unique ability to offer long consecutive barrel sections.

The unique geography of Cloudbreak, with its horseshoe-shaped reef and exposure to south and southwest swells, creates ideal conditions for the formation of these long, consecutive barrels.

The combination of speed, power, and wave shape makes it a coveted destination for surfers from all over the world seeking the thrill of riding double barrels on a single wave.

43

In Hawaii, surfers have taken their passion to the extreme by attempting to surf near active lava flows, a feat that combines adrenaline, danger, and a deep connection with the volcanic nature of the archipelago.

One of the most prominent figures in this field is adventurer and surfer Alison Teal, known for her ecological focus and exploratory spirit.

In 2016, during an eruption of the Kilauea volcano on the Big Island of Hawaii, Alison Teal became the first person to surf waves formed near active lava rivers.

Accompanied by a film crew, she ventured into waters where the incandescent lava met the ocean, generating steam and extremely hazardous conditions.

Her goal was to raise awareness about the fragility of the environment and the need to protect these unique ecosystems.

Teal's feat was not only an act of bravery but also a statement about the interconnectedness between humans and nature.

By surfing in such a hostile environment, she highlighted the importance of respecting and preserving Hawaii's sacred and natural places.

Her achievement was widely publicized and served to inspire others to consider the relationship between adventure and environmental conservation.

In addition to Alison Teal, other local surfers have explored the possibilities of surfing near volcanic areas, though with extreme caution due to the risks involved.

These initiatives have highlighted Hawaii's uniqueness as a place where surf culture and volcanic activity coexist, offering breathtaking yet dangerous settings for lovers of extreme surfing.

44

The earliest surfboards known, used by the ancient inhabitants of Polynesia and especially in Hawaii, were rudimentary but sacred objects, hand-carved from native tree trunks such as koa, wiliwili, or ulu.

They were known as alaia, kikoʻo, and olo, depending on the size and the social class of the surfer.

The olo, for example, were long and exclusive to royalty, reaching up to 5.5 meters in length and weighing between 60 and 70 kilograms due to the density of the wood and the absence of any modern materials to lighten them.

These boards had no fins, meaning they lacked a fixed direction and slid laterally or freely over the wave, making control depend entirely on balance, body positioning, and the surfer's skill.

Surfing with these boards required a technique completely different from today's, closer to the art of gliding and fluidity rather than carving or the abrupt maneuvers seen now.

The finless design forced surfers to use the board's edge, known as the rail, to change direction.

This not only limited the types of maneuvers that could be performed but also made it extremely difficult to stay within the wave's line.

Additionally, the weight made paddling an exhausting task, and any fall carried a high risk of impact.

Nevertheless, these boards were symbols of status and spiritual connection.

The carving of the board, its decoration with oils or shells, and even the selection of the tree from which it was taken, were all performed through ceremonial rituals that honored the gods of the sea and asked permission from nature.

This type of board was used for centuries until colonization and European evangelization suppressed Hawaiian cultural practices, including surfing, which was nearly extinct by the late 19th century.

It was rescued and revitalized in the early 20th century by figures like Duke Kahanamoku, who helped revive and modernize the practice.

Over time, boards evolved with materials like balsa wood, fiberglass, and resin, and in the 1930s, the legendary surfer Tom Blake introduced the first fin, inspired by ship rudders, which radically changed control and maneuverability on the wave.

The transition from those early 70-kg finless boards to today's boards weighing just 2 or 3 kg, with hydrodynamic designs and multiple fin configurations (single fin, twin, thruster, quad, etc.), marks one of the most profound transformations in the history of surfing.

Yet even today, some experimental and traditional surfers return to using finless boards, inspired by those original alaia, seeking to recapture the sensation of flowing without mechanical control, letting themselves be carried by the wave with respect, humility, and pure connection to the ocean.

Because ultimately, that heavy, directionless board of the Polynesian ancestors was not a limitation: it was a way of surrendering to the rhythm of the sea.

45

Cheating, Fixing, and Controversies.

1. Surf Ranch Pro 2023 – Controversial Scoring in Favor of Griffin Colapinto

During the event at Kelly Slater's artificial wave pool in California, American surfer Griffin Colapinto was declared the winner over Brazilian Italo Ferreira. The surfing community, especially in Brazil, denounced a lack of transparency and consistency in the scoring. Top surfers like Gabriel Medina openly criticized the WSL, accusing the panel of judges of favoring local or more "marketable" competitors instead of purely judging performance.

2. Paris 2024 Olympics – Judge Removed for Conflict of Interest

Australian judge Ben Lowe was removed from the judging panel at Teahupo'o, Tahiti, after a photo circulated showing him hugging surfer Ethan Ewing and the Australian coach. Given that Lowe had already faced criticism for bias in previous events, the ISA deemed that his continued participation compromised the event's impartiality. This decision received significant international media coverage and reignited the debate over objectivity in Olympic scoring.

3. Lawsuit Against the WSL – Alexandre Botelho Case at Nazaré

In 2020, Portuguese surfer Alexandre Botelho suffered a severe accident during the Nazaré Tow Challenge and nearly lost his life. He later sued the World Surf League for gross negligence and fraudulent concealment, claiming that conditions were unsafe and that athletes were pressured into signing liability waivers. The case highlighted the fragility of safety protocols at big wave events.

4. Gabriel Medina vs. WSL – Ongoing Accusations of Favoritism

Triple world champion Gabriel Medina has been at the center of multiple complaints against the WSL, especially in heats where decisions favored competitors from other countries, even when their maneuvers were clearly inferior. In several tournaments (such as at Surf Ranch and Tahiti), Medina has openly published criticisms, going so far as to say that the system was "rotten from the inside" and that "politics was winning over surfing."

5. "Ghost Interferences" on Tour

In professional surfing, an "interference" occurs when a surfer blocks another's line on the same wave. There have been cases where unjustified interferences were called, favoring certain surfers at critical moments. Although direct bad faith has rarely been proven, there have been allegations of tactical manipulation by coaches and complicit judges, especially in early rounds where cameras do not capture all angles.

6. Nationality Changes for Qualification Strategy

Some surfers have been questioned for changing their country of representation to gain easier access to international events, such as American surfers with dual nationality competing for nations with fewer qualifying spots, which some consider a strategy "borderline unethical."

7. Phantom Scores in QS Events

In the Qualifying Series circuit, where not all heats are officially broadcast, there have been reports of local surfers receiving unusually high scores in rounds without video coverage, raising suspicions of "compensation" or favoritism by local organizers in countries like Indonesia, Mexico, or Morocco. Some surfers have publicly stated that "there is no guarantee of fairness without cameras."

8. Media Pressure on Judges – Cases of Indirect Manipulation

In events like the Pipe Masters or the Quiksilver Pro France, there have been reports of how judges can be influenced by media pressure and sponsoring brands, favoring surfers with a stronger social media presence or those representing major commercial interests. Kelly Slater himself has mentioned in interviews that "surfing, as a judged sport, is not immune to politics, image, and interests."

9. Scoring Error Acknowledged at the Bonsoy Gold Coast Pro

In 2024, the WSL acknowledged a scoring error at the Bonsoy Gold Coast Pro, where surfer Nat Young received a lower score than he deserved. Although the correction did not change the outcome of the heat, the acknowledgment was seen as a step toward greater transparency in the judging system.

10. Accusations of Bias Against Brazilian Surfers

Brazilian surfers such as Gabriel Medina, Italo Ferreira, and Filipe Toledo have repeatedly expressed concerns over judging decisions they consider unfair. Medina, in particular, has been vocal in his criticisms of the WSL, pointing out scoring inconsistencies and a possible lack of recognition for progressive surfing.

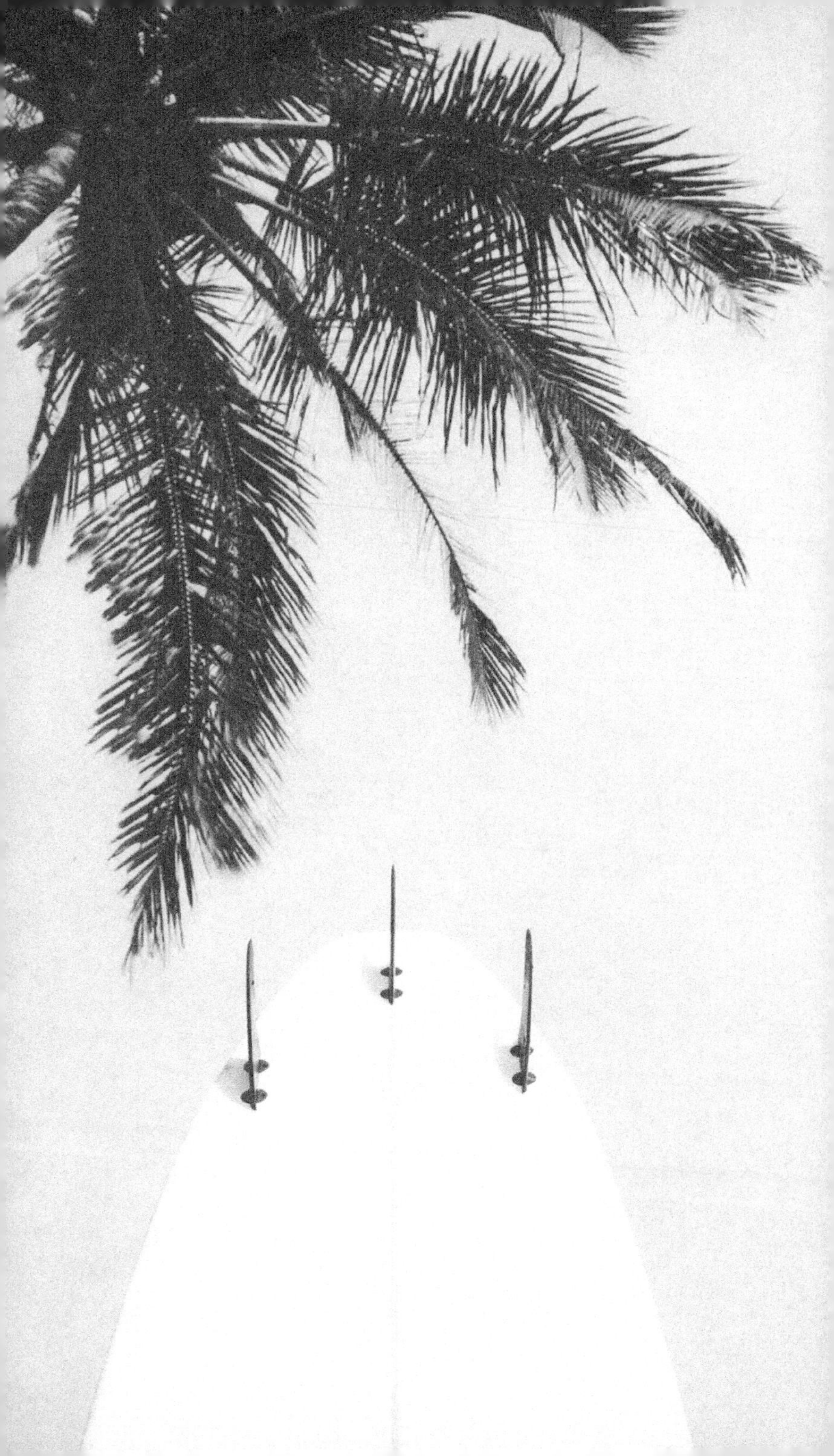

Printed in Great Britain
by Amazon